Billy Moore was born in Liverpool in ... upbringing and struggled with addiction. In 2005, wishing to make a fresh start, he relocated to Thailand and entered a period of sobriety. However, he eventually relapsed and was arrested and charged by Thai police and sent to Klong Prem prison. More recently, Billy has not only survived cancer, but also gone on to become a powerful advocate of boxing and anti-knife crime initiatives in the Liverpool area.

Praise for *Fighting for My Life*

'The next round in Billy's fight is pain-racked, frank and reflective . . .
an inspiring piece from a man who's been to hell and back and has
the scars to prove it'

Joe Cole

'Billy Moore writes with such a tragic authenticity that it kept me
willing for him to succeed, even as I knew he was never too far from
self-destruction. It's his self-awareness that I admire – unflinching
and brutal and also, it should be said, his wonderful way with words'

Professor Emeritus David Wilson, author of
My Life with Murderers

'Brutally honest, dark and disturbing. A book that tells of the reality
of drugs and a failing prison system'

Neil Samworth, author of
Strangeways: A Prison Officer's Story

'His life may have had many ups and downs, but Billy is a wonderful
example of never giving up'

James English

'A true story of forgiveness, not only learning to forgive others but
also learning to forgive yourself. An incredibly emotional story about
an incredible man who's had an incredible journey'

Liam Harrison

Fighting for My Life

A Prisoner's Story of Redemption

Billy Moore

ROBINSON

ROBINSON

First published in Great Britain in 2021 by Robinson
This paperback edition published in 2023 by Robinson

1 3 5 7 9 10 8 6 4 2

A CIP catalogue record for this book
is available from the British Library.

ISBN: 978-1-47214-561-1

Typeset in Bembo by SX Composing DTP, Rayleigh, Essex
Printed and bound in Great Britain by Clays Ltd, Elcograf S.p.A.

Papers used by Robinson are from well-managed forests
and other responsible sources.

Robinson
An imprint of
Little, Brown Book Group
Carmelite House
50 Victoria Embankment
London EC4Y 0DZ

An Hachette UK Company
www.hachette.co.uk

www.littlebrown.co.uk

This book is dedicated to my father Tony Moore and
to my son Albie who I wish my father had met

CONTENTS

Prologue   1

1 Release   5

2 Home   17

3 Desperation   29

4 Detox   33

5 Toxic   47

6 Hurricane   57

7 Paris   71

8 Drifting   77

9 Cancer   81

10 Philippines   89

11 Relapse   99

12 Olivia   107

13 Rob   113

14 Using   117

15 Rehab   127

16 Arrest   139

17 Consequences   145

18 Prison   155

19 Clean   165

20 Malaise   173

21 Badinage   185

22 Moods   201

23 Stitched   213

24 Sabotage   221

25 Reflections   229

26 Happy?   239

Hereafter   *251*

Acknowledgements   255

Index   257

Prologue

CANNES was a playboy's paradise. I enjoyed the scenery and spent my day walking along the beach, reflecting on all I had achieved. The screening was being held at midnight; I got dressed in my tuxedo and felt like James Bond. This was it, my night. We were picked up and taken to the entrance of the cinema in a limousine. I smiled like the Cheshire Cat all the way and I was in a permanent state of excitement. I stepped out of the car to the sound of the Jackson 5's 'ABC' being pumped out loudly from massive speakers. Wow, this was incredible – people cheering, girls screaming. It was a special moment in my life and just ahead lay the massive red carpet.

Cameras flashed and the paparazzi shouted for me to turn their way. It all seemed surreal. That evening my life would be immortalised on the big screen. There was a buzz spread through Cannes like electricity; this was the most prestigious film festival in the calendar and the elite of the entertainment world was there. So was I. I was asked to do a brief interview about my story before being escorted to the red carpet. About ten minutes were spent having our pictures taken and then we were shown into the cinema that was absolutely full to the rafters. There were over two-and-a-half thousand people inside, all smartly dressed, and I was told that this was the biggest cinema in the world. I was greeted with cheers and a round of applause.

The lights went down and the movie began. I was sitting next to Jean, the French film director who was the architect of this amazing piece of cinema. I sat with bated breath. Some scenes were difficult to watch and the movie tapped into my emotional senses. The entire theatre was in deadly silence throughout. The movie ended some two hours later, the lights came back on and then suddenly the whole cinema erupted with screams and yells of approval. I looked around, shocked: everybody was on their feet and we were getting a standing ovation that went on for over eight minutes.

'Is this normal?' I asked.

This was amazing. I felt on top of the world and the next day's reviews were outstanding: we had done it; we had brought my story to life.

But . . . how can one man go from standing in a new tuxedo on a red carpet at the world's most prestigious film festival, with thousands of people clapping and cheering his achievements on a Saturday evening, to a crack den in Liverpool on a Monday morning?

Well, let me tell you the story of one man's fall from grace, his journey from break-ups and make-ups to a battle with cancer and his daily struggle with relapse and abstinence. I had once taken inspiration from Oscar Wilde's wise words that while we are all in the gutter, some of us are looking at the stars. I now knew how it felt to have the tips of my fingers reach into the sky and touch the edge of my dreams. But now, in a defining moment, it felt as if I was experiencing a huge volte-face. I had literally gone from being among the stars to right back in the gutter I had fought so hard to leave behind. This is the story of that journey. It is mine alone to tell.

Chapter 1
Release

Commend me to him: I will send his ransom;
And being enfranchised, bid him come to me.
'Tis not enough to help the feeble up,
But to support him after.

Timon of Athens Act 1, Scene 1,
Thomas Middleton and William Shakespeare

'MOORE A7853AP!'

I could hear my surname and prison number being shouted across the prison sports hall of HMP Wandsworth where I worked as a gym orderly. I had been given a job cleaning the toilets in the gym, which I didn't mind as it was a small price to pay for extra gym sessions – something I needed to cleanse my soul while locked up.

I put away my mop and walked over to the two prison staff who I recognised from my wing, a Mr Davis and Miss Richardson. Both young, both new and both seemed like reasonable human beings. Still I was confused. Why was I being summoned?

The thought of a random drug test crossed my mind but that

didn't worry me as I was sure to be all clear, but as a prisoner you carry with you an enduring suspicion of the authorities. *What have I done?* is a prisoner's default mode. It could never be a good thing, screws turning up at your workplace late in the afternoon to speak to you about something or to take you somewhere you didn't want to go. I wasn't due a visitor, so the time it took me to walk from one end of the sports hall to the other had me thinking all kinds of crazy stuff. The insecure, paranoid thoughts and scenarios I created in my mind would have me locked up and the keys thrown away for good (were anyone able to access them).

Miss Richardson smiled at me as I approached her. Her short blonde hair was tied back in a severe bun, and she had a baby face with chubby cheeks. She was so small in stature I doubted she would be able to handle herself in a kick-off if one ever took place on her shift.

'Moore, pack your kit, you're going home,' she beamed, her cheeks flushing vermillion while Mr Davis nodded along.

'What? Are you being serious?' I was shocked. My sheer disbelief must have been obvious.

'Yes, your paperwork has finally arrived from Thailand . . . today is the day of your release,' said Mr Davis, waving a bunch of papers in his hand. 'Come along then, let's get you to reception and processed.'

It was 4.30 p.m. and I hadn't even had my evening meal! Nervous, I instinctively laughed at the thought of how I would miss out on one final prison slop. This news was truly the last thing I had expected.

I don't think anyone said anything as I was escorted back to the wing to pack up my belongings. If they did, I never heard a word as I was so consumed by my own thoughts. Where would I go? Home? Where was home? It was 2010 and I had been away from England for the last five years. I felt dislocated from everyone. What was I to expect? Should I attack Mr Davis and get more time added to my sentence? At least then I wouldn't have to worry about all of this.

The next thing I knew I was standing outside my open cell with a clear plastic bag and was told I had ten minutes to clear out my personal property. There wasn't much really – just a few letters and a bunch of papers that amounted to the start of the book I had been trying to write about my time spent in prison in Thailand and the incredible journey I had been on.

Finished! Bag packed and my mind still racing with thoughts of the unknown. Being unable to predict my immediate future (something you absolutely take for granted in prison) was making me desperately anxious, fearful and excited all at once. I was taken to the reception area of the prison to be formally discharged from HMP Wandsworth, where I had spent the past eight months since I'd been sent back from Thailand.

Mr Davis and Miss Richardson handed over my paperwork to the officer on the front desk and wished me the best of luck before disappearing back on to the wing to help serve the evening meal I was not sorry to forgo. I didn't feel hungry, only scared. I was handed a pen and asked to sign a few documents that I had to take with me to the probation office.

'Where will you be going to, Moore?' the old, grey-haired officer asked. He obviously hadn't seen the inside of a gym since he first started in the prison service probably decades ago.

I looked at him in confusion. 'Where will I be going?'

'Yes, your address. Where do you want this travel warrant for? I assume you need one,' he pressed.

I had no idea. I hadn't planned for any of this. The only location I could think of was the last place I had been before I had left England for Thailand five years earlier. Somewhere in Bournemouth. I'd had a friend there called Jay who, admittedly, I hadn't seen or heard from in the intervening years. But he was my best bet.

'Bournemouth, sir,' I said with a renewed vigour. 'I would like the travel warrant for Bournemouth.'

'OK, Bournemouth it is,' replied old greyhead as he looked over the top of his glasses at the computer screen. A few minutes passed while he found the nearest probation office that I had to attend before 12 the following day.

'Take a seat, Moore. Someone will come along to escort you out shortly,' he grunted.

'Thanks,' was all I could muster.

This was it! This was the day I had dreamed of for so long, and now here I was sitting on the precipice alone and scared, not wanting to jump. *How ironic*, I thought.

I literally had nowhere certain to go to. No home I could call my own.

It felt like hours before a tall, soft-spoken prison officer, who introduced himself as Officer Goulding, asked me to follow him. I stood up and did what I was told. While my mind was working overtime, my body moved without volition, conditioned by years of obeying instructions given by officers both here and in Thailand.

'There you go now, be on your way,' Officer Goulding said, pointing to the open door that led, incredibly, to the outside world. Like a zombie I walked forward and didn't look back; it's a bad omen to look back at a prison as you leave – something you are never supposed to do.

The looming prison gates were firmly shut, but the small, head-high door swung open on its well-oiled hinges and I was ushered on to the streets outside HMP Wandsworth with my bag of clothes, a few letters and a one-way ticket to Bournemouth. I heard the door slam shut behind me. I had long fantasised about this precise moment but now, for what seemed like an eternity, I stood rooted to the spot, confused about what to do next.

I had no phone or numbers to call even if I had one. All I could hope for was to find my only friend Jay and the only place I knew where to look for him was the Happy Health Spa in Bournemouth. The place was basically a swingers' club owned by a fat ponce called Vito the Frog. Vito looked a bit grubby, and had greasy hair and frog-like features.

I had a discharge grant of a few pounds that I used to hire a cab to the club from Bournemouth train station. The door to the club was open so I made my way in. The reception desk was unmanned and I could hear a disco beat belting out of speakers coming from upstairs. There were other noises, a lot like loud grunts and somebody being whacked with a stick . . . I slowly crept up the stairs and, as I did, the grunts got louder. I inched nearer to a half-closed door, the room beyond illuminated by a dim, red-shaded light, and gently pushed it open. I couldn't believe what I saw: there was Vito, the fat ponce, in a rubber gimp suit with a solid ball gag in his mouth. On his back was a young Filipino girl wearing a Stetson, hitting him with a horse crop, screaming, 'Yee-haw!' at the top of her voice. Vito, understandably preoccupied, took a while before he eventually looked up and our eyes locked uncomfortably. Right there and then I could see his shame. He suddenly performed an impressive buckaroo, throwing the young Filipino girl high into the air from where she landed on her arse with a loud thud. The small, untidy room had a green rubber mattress on the floor and the smell of sex and body odour assaulted my nostrils. The girl scrambled to her feet, screamed something that I didn't understand, spat copiously at Vito and stormed out of the room.

Vito carefully removed the gag and nodded towards the door. 'Alright, Bill, you caught me at bad time there, son.' The shame was still visible in his face.

'Whatever turns you on, mate,' I said, smiling at his discomfort. 'I'm looking for Jay. Do you know where I can find him?'

'I ain't seen him in years, son. As matter of fact, I ain't seen you around for a while. How you been?'

'I've been worse.'

'Fancy a cuppa tea, my old son?'

'I haven't got time for pleasantries. Do you know how I can get hold of him, you fat fuck?' I spat angrily, losing my patience with this fucking pervert.

'OK, OK. No need for that. Have a word with the staff downstairs. Someone might know how to get hold of him. I'm sorry I can't help you,' he said, shrugging his shoulders.

I left him standing there in the shiny, rubber gimp suit he'd somehow poured himself into. The place was as seedy as ever. It was getting late and I had nothing in the way of accommodation arranged. Last night, I had slept in a prison bed. Tonight, I was bedless. There was absolutely nothing in place for me upon release. It was becoming one nightmare after another. What was I supposed to do?

Before leaving the club, I asked a young bikini-clad girl serving drinks if she had ever heard of a guy called Snowy. He'd worked in the club for years, and she fortunately knew who he was and had his telephone number. She pointed me in the direction of a scabby-looking payphone in a dingy corner of the club. *Brilliant*, I thought, *things are improving*. I managed to get Snowy on the phone. He wasn't the sharpest tool in the box, but he was a loyal enough guy who worked hard and actually had Jay's number. Scrabbling for change, I called my old friend for some support.

'Hello, my son, where are you? Are you all right? Fuck me, Bill, it's beautiful to hear from you,' he boomed in his cockney accent.

For the first time since my release I felt like someone cared. The genuine concern I could detect in Jay's voice relieved me of some of the anxiety. I had been feeling overwhelmed by everything since I had been let out of prison. Jay gave me his address and promised to pay for the cab journey.

Sadly, certain people, places and things could not be avoided and living with my friend Jay, who was using drugs at the time, was a disaster waiting to happen. He was what you would call a functioning addict: he had a roof over his head, a good job and a Mercedes on the drive but had fallen into the age-old trap of dealing drugs to support his habit.

I managed to resist temptation for a while, but it wasn't long before I was back in the grip of addiction and with no one to blame but myself. I justified anything that would block out the memories of what I'd been through while I was banged up in a Thai prison. I'd received PTSD counselling while in HMP Wandsworth via a Mr Thoroughgoode (you couldn't make it up), a ponytailed male therapist with a degree in asking trendy, 'so right-on', deep-meaning-bullshit questions. In between showing me shitty card tricks, he would come out with things like, 'Hi Billy, what would you do if a pink elephant appeared in this room?' He'd said this leaning towards me with a look of earnestness that got my hackles up every time.

'I would shoot it, of course,' I replied, a little bit taken aback.

'Hmm, I see. Guns, shooting . . . can I ask you where you would get the weapon from, Billy?' he asked while jotting down something in his black leather notepad.

'I'd get the weapon from the same place you got your fucking pink elephant,' I said as I walked out in disgust.

I'd just come back from three years in the most barbaric prison on earth where I had nearly died on several occasions from disease, getting stabbed and beaten . . . and this numpty with his ridiculous virtue-signalling ponytail was doing card tricks and talking about pink elephants. What the actual fuck . . . ?

So that was a good enough reason, among a long list of other bullshit reasons I had, to help fuel my self-destructive behaviour. I'd drifted through society with the wind blowing through my soul; the years had passed me by in the blink of an eye and so I began writing down my experiences of loss and pain. I had so desperately wanted to stay clean, but it had proved impossible in the circles I mixed in. My thoughts haunted me and I would live in the drugged-up landscape of my mind more often than I did in reality. The overwhelming loneliness was torture. To explain how I felt was hard. Even being surrounded by people couldn't take away the desperate feeling of emptiness. Not even a woman's love had the power to remove the fear of impending loss and loneliness. Girlfriends didn't hang about long; I was too difficult to be around. My life became as barren as my thoughts.

I wasn't happy with my surroundings, but had nowhere else to go. Girlfriends came and went. I stayed indoors alone and wrote a lot about growing up on the streets of Liverpool and my three-year nightmare of being locked up in Thailand. I was searching for an answer as to what was wrong with me. This was all I had: a story, my story, but who would be interested in reading about me anyway? Doubt crept in. The last time I had attempted to write anything about myself was when I was twenty-five years old and banged up with an Irish guy named Terry Jenkins (who died of an overdose many years later). I remember lying on my bunk in Stafford prison dreaming about writing a book. I spoke of my future goal to Terry who popped his head down from the top bunk, looked sternly at me and said in no uncertain terms, 'Who the fuck is going to read a book about you, ye feckin' eejit? You've done nothing but smoke heroin and come to jail. No offence, but you might as well give up now.' He laughed so hard he nearly bust a rib. That was the end of that dream.

Now, ten years later, I'd smoked even more heroin, been to jail yet again, but had packed in a hell of a lot of living in too. Bollocks to you, Terry. I was going to write that book. The people in the education department of HMP Wandsworth, who had encouraged me to write, well, they'd believed in me!

Despite my writing, my dependence on drugs was by now all-consuming: my life in Bournemouth began to deteriorate fast, mentally and physically. I am ashamed to admit it, but I began using intravenously, injecting more misery and pain into my body, past caring. This ultimately put me in hospital. While there, I met Larry-the-handbag who was in the bed next to me. Overweight and pasty-looking, he wheezed like Darth Vader on a chilly damp morning. In his sixties, with his posh accent and all the airs and graces, he came across as a likeable old-school toff.

As we chatted and I told him about my plans to turn my life story into a book, he became friendly with me, helping me out with a few pounds here and there. Well, I couldn't refuse his generosity; the money went straight to fund my ongoing drug habit. Who in addiction would have refused? Larry was obviously well educated and helped a bit with my writing – coming up with some good tips and the occasional word the *Oxford English Dictionary* would be proud of. As our friendship grew, he suggested he should become my agent and would make arrangements to open a joint bank account. He had apparently represented quite a few celebrities over the years. With my usually streetwise brain half-wasted owing to the liberal amount of heroin I was using, I just nodded benignly, agreeing to his great idea.

Just a couple of days later, as I dozed in the patients' lounge watching *News at Ten*, who should feature in one of the evening's lead stories but 'Larry-agent-to-the-fucking-stars'.

'Larry-conman-of-the-fucking-stars' more like. He'd only been caught up in a newspaper sting on a senior politician and, as I discovered, had a well-earned reputation as a scam artist. Despite my grudging admiration for his talents as a charlatan, I decided Larry wasn't quite the agent I was looking for. Another relationship I consigned to the bin.

In the end, all I wanted was to go and see my mother. I felt so alienated and distant from society; the years I had spent away had chipped away at my soul. I had exhausted all avenues and burned all bridges. All that was left was the unconditional love of a mother. I padded along the corridor in my hospital gown and slippers and called her number from a payphone.

'Hello, Mum, are you OK? It's me, Billy,' I said. Tears were stinging my eyes.

'Oh Billy, where are you? Why haven't you been home to see me? Are you OK, son?' she said lovingly, deep concern in her voice.

'Hmm, yep, I'm fine,' I said, remaining tight-lipped and afraid to talk, knowing my voice would break.

'Come home, son. We miss you,' she said. Her sadness was all too obvious.

'I'm on my way,' I said, ending the call. A painful lump had formed in my throat and I felt exposed and embarrassed as patients and nurses passed by in the corridor. The decision had been made; this was a positive step in the right direction. I was going home to give my mother a big, loving hug.

My mother Pat was one of sixteen children and her own mother had killed herself when I was six or seven years old. Mum was small but tough. She had to be to bring up six children virtually on her own while my father spent most of his time in the boozer or betting office, throwing away what little money we had. I remember vividly the screams from my mum as my father beat her. I was really small and physically unable to protect her, and I would cover my ears with my hands and squeeze tightly to muffle the abuse hurled her way. My mother worked really hard and I would help out by cleaning up and making all the beds – we all chipped in back then and helped out. Even at an early age I was looking for acceptance and approval.

Every Sunday afternoon we would have a tea party, with homemade cakes, jellies, assorted biscuits and pop. It was the only time my five younger siblings and I would laugh and play fight with each other. Then it was bath time. I would share a bath with my younger brother Anthony, leaving the water for Joe and Kevin. My mother would then refill the bath for my baby sisters, Kelly and Lisa. Finally, the nit comb would be dragged through our hair; we all took turns, with both my sisters squealing every time they had their hair done. I would tease and pull faces at our Kelly, the elder of my two sisters, causing her to shout to my mum and tell her I was laughing at her. I would get a slap for that, but it was never hard.

I remember holding my mum's hand one evening as we walked to her friends. She was about twenty-five years old at the time and was crying. I never really saw my mum cry but I knew the reason for her distress was my father.

'I'll never be like my dad. I promise, Mum,' I said, tightly squeezing her hand.

'I know. You're a good boy, Billy,' she said, looking down at me and smiling through her tears.

Chapter 2

Home

As a decrepit father takes delight
To see his active child do deeds of youth,
So I, made lame by Fortune's dearest spite,
Take all my comfort of thy worth and truth;

Sonnet XXXVII, William Shakespeare

M Y mother looked at me for the first time in six years and knew immediately there was something wrong. There was no hiding the haunted look of desperation on my face. The empty shell of a man standing before her was not the man who had confidently left for a short holiday all those years ago. I stared into my poor mother's eyes and saw the years of pain she too had suffered. The lines on her face denoted decades of hardship. My mother brought us up in an era of difficult times and, although she worked hard in low-paid jobs, had to rely on benefits and council housing support. Nevertheless, our mother loved each and every one of us and did her best to make sure we all had clothes on our backs and enough food on the table. One Christmas she had asked me what I wanted for a present and, to her surprise, I said I wanted weights.

'Weights?! Why weights, son? Don't you want a bike like your friends?' I told her I didn't and that I wanted weights and that was all. She looked down at me while holding my chin in her soft hands and asked again, 'Are you sure, son? Why do you want weights? You're only six.' She squeezed both my cheeks with a loving smile on her face.

'I want to be big and strong so I can protect you,' I told her. The tears began to fall down both our faces as she pulled me close to her, hugging me tight.

It was October 1979 and I had lost my grandmother in July of that year. It was the first time I can remember any kind of sadness invading my life. My mother allowed me to stay up one evening while my dad was out drinking. She wanted to pop over the road to her friend for a cuppa and told me to watch TV for a while. The living-room curtains were wide open and it was pitch black outside. If they were to look in, people walking past our home would have seen a young child sitting alone. There was a *Carry On* movie playing on the TV and I was engrossed in it. Out of the corner of my eye I noticed something move, and turned towards the window. It was the curtains: they were closing by themselves and I sat rooted to the spot, frightened to move. Eventually I succeeded in jumping up, terrified, and ran upstairs as fast as I could to wake my younger brother, Anthony. He put his head under the blanket when I told him what had just happened. I slowly crept back downstairs. The curtains were open again and, as I stared at them transfixed, my mother walked in.

'Mum, Mum, the curtains have just closed all by themselves,' I panted, excited and terrified at the same time. She didn't even bat an eyelid and told me not to worry – that it was my grandmother looking out for me. On the day she had died, a picture we had hanging up in our hallway fell and broke; moments later there was a knock on the door and there standing in the doorway was my uncle

18

Freddie with a solemn look upon his face. Those seconds are engraved on my mind as if it happened yesterday. I was six years old and not yet corrupted by drugs, and I had definitely felt a presence that evening.

I was called, among other things, a tramp by the other kids in my year at school, just because I didn't wear Farah trousers or Ben Sherman shirts. I always found myself in trouble and standing in front of the head teacher, Mr Connor, who looked eerily like Count Dracula. He was a vicious individual who clearly enjoyed the regular opportunities to give me the cane and would then nastily pinch the back of my naked leg, which hurt! This was the 1970s and teachers got away with a lot more back then. Corporal punishment was both frequent and the norm. Once, when only a little boy, I was away on a school trip that Mum had scrimped and saved for. As we readied for bed and drank bitter-tasting cocoa, a teacher made us all remove our underwear. He claimed it was more hygienic. The rest of the boys and I could see all the way up the girls' nightdresses – the teacher could too. While corporal punishment was flagrant, routine and even encouraged, sexual abuse was also prevalent, but kept under the radar to maintain a veneer of respectability.

My father was a brute of a man who drank too much alcohol; his fists did the talking in our household. With the selective memory of a small child wishing for better, my earliest memories weren't of a drunken man: they were happy loving memories of a man who worked hard and came home to his family at the end of the day. He would pick up both me and my younger brother in his big strong arms, smothering us in love and kisses and blowing raspberries on our tummies. I remember giggling and looking forward to seeing my dad come home from work, waiting excitedly at the innocent age of four. Perhaps those memories are seen through a small boy's rose-tinted glasses, but certainly by the time I was eight years old the atmosphere in the household had started to change. My grandad Frank lived with us for a few years back then: he was old school, a thief who spent most of his life in and out of prison. With an old punch ball and mitts, he taught me boxing and in the process became something of a surrogate father. My dad stopped playing with us and would constantly have a can of lager by his side; he wouldn't even speak to us but would just shout out demands. We always got sent to bed early and I hated the closing theme tune to the 1970s soap *Crossroads* because that was when my father would always shout, 'One, two, three, B. E. D,' to Anthony, my sister Kelly and me. It was still light and you could hear the neighbours' children outside playing while we lay silently in bed in abject misery.

Whatever my dad was going through, he never shared it with anyone. He was angry most of the time. Sometimes we would see him in a jolly mood but that was only after he had been out on a drinking binge. The atmosphere at home became frightening. I was beaten on a regular basis and forced to stand in a corner with my hands on my head, scared of when the next slap would come. I got used to the beatings, if one can ever get used to something like that, but what I feared more than anything was when the next beating would come, the unpredictability. I began to withdraw mentally, and my schooling took a nosedive. I was placed in the 'dumb classes', as they were called back then, and regularly caned by the head teacher. I was in a state of constant anxiety and hated my father by this time.

I'm ten years old and my mother has just been beaten to a pulp; my grandad is old and feels powerless to intervene. My dad is going ballistic because his tea is cold and the house is getting smashed up. He falls into a deep, drunken sleep on the sofa while my mother is hiding upstairs crying and my younger siblings are cowering silently in their bedrooms. I sit on the stairs listening to his loud snores and my thoughts are murderous. I go downstairs into the kitchen and pick up a large kitchen knife that my mother uses to chop vegetables. I slowly creep into the living room and his snores are getting louder with each step. My father is lying on his back. A cigarette has burned down in his nicotine-stained fingers; his glasses have slipped to one side of his face. I walk towards him, carefully watching the rise and fall of his chest in case I disturb his drunken stupor. He's a big man with a handlebar moustache that makes him resemble Thomas Magnum P.I. I want to end his life, end our misery. Fear suddenly grips me. *What if I don't succeed and he wakes up?* There would be hell to pay. I stand there staring at him, hardly daring to breathe for what seems like an age, with the knife clenched tightly in my small hand. I couldn't do it and ran from my father and into the back room, collapsing on to my knees and sobbing wretchedly. I was ten years old and this is what my life had become.

Growing up in the early 1980s was a struggle: the constant physical abuse I was subjected to at home by my father also followed me from primary to secondary school. The beatings became the norm. I got used to getting punched and kicked not only by the man I called my father but also by the gang of youths I had to pass on the way to school every single *fucking* day. I felt like I wore a sign on my forehead that said I'm here to get abused and battered by the rest of society. I never felt like I belonged anywhere in particular and always felt different – somehow separated from the rest of the kids in my area. I was a loner, a 'ronin'. I couldn't understand why I never had a single friend; life was fucking lonely in my world.

Living under the same roof as my father was uncomfortable and the dynamics at home had me spending most of my time on the streets. Drugs and crime started to play a big part in my life. I began to lose interest in boxing, which is something I have regretted for a long time. I initially joined a local boxing club to impress my dad.

The gym was called the St Ambrose ABC. It was small and quite basic compared to what's on offer at most boxing clubs today. I remember my first visit – feeling nervous and not a little frightened. The first thing I noticed was the smell of stale sweat and the persistent loud, intimidating grunts from the handful of boxers in the room. The walls were adorned with tattered and faded posters of great fighters: Leon Spinks, James 'Bonecrusher' Smith and the greatest of all, Muhammad Ali. I was transfixed as I watched a group of older lads working out on ancient, battered leather punchbags, hitting them with solid thwacks and only stopping to rest when a bell sounded. Steam was rising from their hot bodies like overworked racehorses. I was introduced to the coach, John, who wore a warm smile across his ancient-looking, wrinkled and leathery face that looked like it had lived in the ring for most of its life. Not having any money and unable to purchase even a pair of cheap boxing mitts, I was given some second-hand boxing attire to get me started. I was delighted with the kindness shown, the guidance I received, and it felt good to be a part of something. I trained hard three times a week and ran in between sessions to build up my stamina.

My first sparring session was in an old, worn-out boxing ring that was basically a canvas spread across the floor. I kept my guard high; it had been the only way I could protect myself from my father's blows so that was something I had learned before even stepping into the ring. The smell of old sweat that permeated the dog-eared gloves held close to my face felt comforting in a strange sort of way.

I attended the gym regularly and built up friendships with a few of the boys of my own age. It was the first time in my young life that I felt good about something and I was comfortable in the presence of a group of friends whose company I actually enjoyed.

In the same year I joined the club, 1986, Mike Tyson became the youngest-ever world heavyweight champion, and I would creep out of bed in the early hours, while my mother and father slept, to watch his televised fights. I would be in the front room of our house mimicking his moves. Boxing was big on TV throughout the 1980s, unlike today when most of it is behind a paywall, so I enjoyed the privilege of watching all the greats of the decade: Chris Eubank, Michael Watson, Nigel Benn and Frank Bruno. That said, my favourite boxer of all time has to be Roberto 'Hands of Stone' Duran. His fights with Sugar Ray Leonard were legendary, especially the '*No Más*' (No More) battle when Duran refused to fight after the eighth round due to Leonard dancing around too much to avoid getting hit by the hands of stone. What I loved about Duran was his heart and fighting spirit, and how he also came from a poor background to be a world-class boxer.

Boxing became my life and I studied everything about it. I particularly loved watching the *Rocky* movies; Sylvester Stallone was another of my heroes and many years later I got to work with him on the set of *Rambo IV*!

The 1980s were great. We never had much and we enjoyed simple things like cheesy action movies, pop groups and bunking on the bus. The Toxteth riots had an impact on Liverpool as did the Hillsborough disaster, but both brought the city together as a community. Margaret Thatcher was prime minister and following the Argentinean invasion of the Falkland Islands, Britain found itself at war. At the time, certainly in Liverpool, everyone seemed to hate Margaret Thatcher. All I can recall about her is that she took away our milk from school and made everyone angry.

None of what was going on during that decade had any importance to me. All I wanted to do was become a boxer and maybe even join the British Army to escape the life I was living. I joined the Royal Artillery cadets at the weekends but got kicked out after a few months for fighting. But I continued with my boxing.

My first fight was coming up after almost a year of hard training. Excited, I ran home to tell my dad the good news, expecting him to be overjoyed. But it was not to be. My dad just sat there watching the TV in his armchair with a can of lager by his side and a cigarette in his right hand.

'OK son, if you don't knock him out in the first round, I'll knock you out,' he said as he sat there, flicking ash into a big glass ashtray. Stunned, I left.

The fight went ahead, and I didn't win by knocking the guy out in the first round, but I did manage to stop him in the second. As I started to win more boxing competitions, the need for acceptance from my father soon diminished. I was being noticed and respected by the lads in my area, but I was also receiving attention from a few local girls.

My behaviour became reckless as I started to stand on street corners with the same group of thugs who used to attack me on the way to school; how ironic. Drink, drugs and stealing cars became a nightly pattern to fuel the excitement I craved. I desperately wanted to fit in and be a part of something – maybe even find a family among my new comrades, but, as they say, bad company corrupts good character and I was already on the road to ruin. I got myself into a lot of street fights and quickly realised I could fight back with my boxing skills. No longer would I get beaten up without standing up for myself. Not only had I been on the receiving end of violence for the best part of my life, it had now become conditioned within me to deliver it to others. My father ruled our household and bullied me until I was well into my teens, but as I grew older and stronger, I felt more confident about taking care of myself.

I remember when I was about fourteen years old climbing into our neighbours' backyard to take a short cut to the local shop. Mrs McGarrick came out of her back door screaming when she saw me scuttling past. Even though I had my hood up she recognised me.

'Hey you, get out of my garden, you little bastard. I'll be speaking to your father,' I heard her shout at my retreating back.

When I eventually came home my father was waiting for me, his face full of fear and red with anger. The McGarricks were not to be messed with on our estate and had a violent reputation, and I was pretty sure the mother had threatened my father with a hiding from her eldest son.

He grabbed me by the throat and pinned me to the wall, spittle spewing angrily from his mouth.

'You little bastard. You know whose backyard you've just been in, don't you?' he screamed.

I don't know what came over me at that moment, but I reacted and pushed my father away until he fell hard on his backside. He sat there shocked, not saying a word, and for the first time I saw sadness in his eyes. He still said nothing, just pushed himself up off the floor and walked back into the front room. I found myself standing in the hallway alone, not feeling strong or confident but ashamed and embarrassed. It was odd because I started to feel guilt and compassion at the same time. I realised at that moment that my father was human and not the monster I had feared for so long.

Nothing was said about what happened that evening, but it was the last time he laid a finger on me and my mother or anyone else in the family. It didn't stop him from ranting and raving about his dinner being cold or not having any ale money, but it was a lot better than getting beaten on a regular basis.

I was sixteen years old when I had my ear bitten off. It all started with me and a group of friends stealing yet another car from the Liverpool area. In the boot was a big box of Easter eggs. There was a six-foot-tall bully who demanded we hand over the box of goodies. No one wanted to stand up to him, but I did. I told him we would share them out equally, which I thought was fair. He wanted them all. I stood up to him and a fight broke out in my friend's home. Being small I struggled, but managed to hit him with a good few punches, knocking him back into the wall. All he could do was wrestle and hold on to me. He pulled me to his chest and with my left ear exposed he bit into it and held on. I pulled away fast and, in doing so, tore half of my ear off. I was under the influence of LSD at the time, so everything seemed a bit unreal. He ran out of the house and my friend's mother called for an ambulance. The surgery to repair my left ear didn't work.

My mother spent decades suffering at the hands of my father until eventually she found the courage to kick him out. By then I was an adult and the damage had already been done. The many years of suffering from low self-esteem and being treated badly by my father had propelled my addiction even further.

It took many years to find the forgiveness for what he had put us through. Some of my younger siblings didn't see the nasty, bullying side to him that I did, and for that I am grateful. In his later years, I still knew nothing of his background or upbringing, but we developed a relationship and I found a way to learn to love him. He was kind and loving to his youngest daughter Lisa and doted on her children; he still loved my mother and I believe he regretted his mistakes. He had stopped drinking in the last four years of his life; I would visit him once a week in his little bedsit and spend an hour or two with him. Not much was said between us; the silence was enough. I just wish he had been a father to me all those years ago and had allowed me to be a carefree child, full of life. When he passed away in hospital, he had his whole family around him. We held his hand as he took his final breath and I let him go with love.

I don't want to portray my father in a bad light. He had his problems and his crosses to bear, and he just didn't know where to get help or that he needed it. I am grateful that nowadays there's a place for the likes of me to go to and talk about how we feel. We all have our addictions – wet or dry, they both make you high. I have learned it is never the actual drink or drug that should bear the blame, it's where it took you that's the problem.

All I want you to understand is that at no point did I ever wake up one morning and decided to commit crime and become a heroin addict. I had dreams of becoming a championship boxer or joining the British Army. For years, not only have I been beaten up at home, on the streets, on prison landings and in the boxing ring, I have beaten myself up too. And I have continued to do so for most of my life. I did things I didn't want to do and found myself in places I didn't want to be. I'm not a victim – or maybe I am, but if so, I am a victim of myself. I wish with all my heart to help make a difference in the lives of others one day.

When I went up to Liverpool from Bournemouth to see her, my mother had literally aged before my eyes; she looked tired and worn out from the years of stress and worry. I wanted to hold her and give her a huge hug, but something stopped me. It was an uncomfortable feeling that I recognised as the fear of rejection. This was something I had experienced over the years that had me sabotaging all my relationships; it was a pattern I needed to break. There was a deep sense of loss, the missed years, the relationship between us fractured. As she sobbed at the sight of her eldest son who stood before her, I was absolutely broken and felt deep shame.

'It's OK, Mum, I'm going to be all right.' I immediately regretted my selfishness, thinking of my feelings ahead of hers.

She was inconsolable, and it was painful to see her this way. She knew I was using drugs – what kind of drugs didn't really matter, but she knew I was taking something. I lied and told her it was just the medication; the denial was ingrained in me. I moved into my mother's home with her partner and his two children. It was difficult and uncomfortable and you could cut the atmosphere with a knife. I shared a room with my younger brother Joe, who is autistic. He was always smiling but anger and self-hatred permeated my life. Nothing about me was smiling and nothing outside of me could change that.

Chapter 3

Desperation

That we should, with joy, pleasure, revel and applause,
transform ourselves into beasts!

Othello Act 2, Scene 3, William Shakespeare

LIFE consisted of struggling to get out of bed and take the daily short walk to the chemist to collect my methadone, constantly sweating with anxiety. One cold, wet September morning I was walking my route as usual, wearing shorts and flip-flops and consumed by thoughts of getting and using, and finding the ways and means to get hold of more drugs. Looking at the ground, avoiding eye contact with anyone, all I saw was the feet of the people who passed me by. I was embarrassed and ashamed of the monster I had become, the man I should have or could have been had long gone; this fucking addiction was robbing the spirit that had once flourished and was destroying the simple enjoyment of living.

Beep-beep. A loud horn sounded from a white van that suspiciously pulled up next to me. I didn't stop and carried on walking, thinking it probably wasn't for me anyway. I picked up my pace, fixedly staring at the pavement as I marched on. *BEEEEEP* . . . Now the horn sounded for longer and harder. Whoever it was, they were definitely trying to get my attention. *This can't be good*, I thought.

'Billy, is that you?' someone shouted. 'It is you. How are you, lad? I haven't seen you for years, how the devil are you?' a voice shouted insistently.

Stopping, I looked up to see a bald head and familiar face: it was Podge, an old friend from Narcotics Anonymous.

'Where are you going, lad? Do you need a lift anywhere? What the fuck are you wearing flip-flops for? You're not in Thailand any more,' said Podge, looking with distaste at the state of me while the incessant Liverpool rain streamed down my face. I opened the passenger door and jumped in with gratitude. The look in Podge's eyes was a mixture of pity and concern; he was a good man who, like me, had struggled for many years in the grip of addiction. However, over time he had managed to find recovery and build a new life with a beautiful family. Podge was in his late forties and always had time for the struggling addict. He extended the hand of friendship to those who were willing to change, offering his support.

'What's been going on with you, Billy? You look like shit!' said Podge, as we drove towards the chemist. 'When did you get out of that prison in Thailand? I heard all about it, it must've been hell for you. What are you doing with yourself now? Obviously using by the look of it. Have you got somewhere to stay?' he said, constantly firing questions at me. 'Are you on a script? How heavy's your using, mate?' He carried on – a relentless barrage of questions.

'I'm on eighty mils of methadone,' I said, burning up with shame.

He looked at me like I was crazy, which wasn't far from the truth, and offered to take me to a Narcotics Anonymous meeting. Desperate for some normality, I immediately said yes. Some kind of intervention was needed and it had arrived in the guise of my old friend Podge.

I waited all day for the meeting to start, anxious and excited at the same time. He picked me up at 7 p.m. and I was still amazed that seven years on he had remained clean and in recovery; it gave me enormous hope that the same could be possible for me. My mother smiled at me for the first time since I had arrived; she was pleased I was making the effort even if it was a small first step.

The meeting was Podge's home group. It was small but intimate and well attended by the regulars. I was nervous and felt vulnerable. It had been a long time since I'd been to a meeting and most of my early recovery was based in Bristol back in 2004 so this was new territory.

'Have you thought about getting off the meth, Billy?' Podge asked on the drive to the meeting. 'Have you had enough, lad? There's a new way of life, you do know that don't you?' he said softly.

'I know. It's killing my mum to see me like this. I've had enough,' I managed to mumble through clenched teeth. Podge glanced at me as he continued driving, but said nothing.

'I've got an allergy to drugs. I don't break out in lumps and bumps. I break out in handcuffs, misery, pain and loss,' I said in a feeble attempt at humour. And then, hanging my head in shame, admitted that it wasn't a joke: that really was how I was feeling.

'We can help you, but you need to meet us halfway,' Podge said.

'I want it. I'm just frightened of failure. The thought of those long sleepless nights, the sweats and the cramps scares the shit out of me,' I said, feeling the emotion building up.

'They're the consequences we have to face. If taking drugs was easy, nobody would want to stop,' said Podge. 'You only have to rattle once. It's not fun – I know, I've been there – but when we get clean, we never have to use again. One day at a time,' he said, passion flooding his voice.

The sudden realisation I wasn't alone dawned on me. My chest began to heave as I sobbed silently, the tears falling freely. Podge looked over at me, not out of pity but with a solemn sense of under-standing. I welcomed the silence that existed between us: it wasn't an awkward silence, it was the therapeutic value of one lost soul helping another. We arrived at the meeting and entered the small room. It was full of people chatting and some even laughed with one another, while others sat alone, clearly deep in thought. A young girl, no older than twenty-five, welcomed me to the group and gave me the best hug ever. She offered me a drink. I sat down feeling like a fraud because I was still using even though I knew the only requirement for membership was a desire to stop. I felt envious of the other people in the room: they looked fresh, happy and alive with no worries or burdens. I began to judge and compare their stories to my own. Their using had to be a tea party compared to mine, I told myself. Shit! I was already separating myself and looking for differences before I had even given myself a chance. Podge looked at me and gave me a knowing wink. It was good to know he was there in my corner; he helped me a lot in those early days. The meeting ended and everybody told me to keep coming back.

Chapter 4
Detox

'This is no flattery: these are counsellors
That feelingly persuade me what I am.'
Sweet are the uses of adversity,
Which, like the toad, ugly and venomous,
Wears yet a precious jewel in his head.

As You Like It Act 2, Scene 1,
William Shakespeare

THE term 'detox' has been hijacked by the peddlers of diet pills and vitamin supplements as a benign, almost pleasant experience to flush out a few toxins derived from over-indulgence. Detox from heroin, crack cocaine or their highly addictive cousins is an arduous, terrifying and desperate battle against fearsome and mighty powerful enemies: emotional, physical and psychological need. Only an addict survivor of the detox war can have any conception of the enormity of the challenge.

If I wanted funding for detox, I needed to engage and show willingness with my drug worker, Leanne. She was young, quite pretty and keen but, critically, was lacking in experience. There was a local detox facility in Liverpool called the Kevin White Unit, and if I really wanted help, Leanne could make a referral for government funding. I would be placed on the waiting list so long as I kept providing negative urine results. I was grateful for her support and hoped I wouldn't have to wait too long. And two weeks later a bed became available. I was ready: I had my bag packed with a few bits and bobs and had been given a time and a date on which to arrive at the unit. Enough was enough, it was now or never. And with only the insane logic of a true addict, I smoked a few joints and had a bit of meth in advance. My ironic way of readying myself to change my life.

I arrived early at the unit. I had no idea what to expect once I walked through the doors. I only wanted to be normal. I had notions of falling in love, getting a job and living life without the constant use of drugs merely to function. In reality, I knew how to recover, knew there was a better way of living and had experienced recovery before. Over the years I had taken my foot off the sanity pedal and allowed other things like money and women to become more important – but I'm not blaming anyone else. The obsessive trait of my personality had led to my relapsing. But now, plucking up the courage, I took a deep breath and pressed the doorbell.

I was greeted by a middle-aged woman who introduced herself as Anne. She had a kind face that broke into a warm, welcoming smile. I sat down and was offered a drink. I took the opportunity to take a look around the reception room. Tatty posters offered advice about how to inject safely and about using condoms. Other posters solemnly warned about HIV, hepatitis and every other sexually transmitted disease, some of whose lurid symptoms made a regular dose of the clap seem hardly worth worrying about. I sat there feeling deeply anxious, afraid I might fail when my name was called.

A door was buzzed open for me and I walked through. The unit was becoming more like a prison as I went on. Were they trying to keep us from escaping and using drugs? I was led into a wide-open room that had a couple of old, minging sofas and a huge TV hanging on the wall. In the corner, pool and table-tennis tables leaned drunkenly. I could see, through a pair of grubby French doors, a beaten-up garden which was currently being used by a couple of groups of people to smoke. Miss Methadone and Miss Crack Cocaine, wearing make-up that looked like it had been applied with a brickie's trowel in the dark, and tarted up in designer label Primark, were sharing a handrolled cigarette, cackling like geese. They were looking in my direction and nudging each other, eyeing me up like I was on the menu in a crack house. What was happening here? Please God tell me I hadn't pulled . . . I was desperately looking for an escape route when my ear was assaulted by a grating, over-loud voice.

'Hello, Billy. How are you, mate?' It was a guy I vaguely recognised from my past. I couldn't recall his name and needed prompting.

'It's me, lad. Yozza. I used to live facing you on Rosebery Road. The Bear's Paw boozer. Ring any bells?' he said, scratching a scab on his bottom lip. He had hawk-like features with high cheekbones, long, brown, scraggy hair and stank like the inside of a wheelie bin.

I did distantly recall him and then remembered what a scaly lizard he was. He was what you would call a grifter, not a grafter, a ponce who bummed off brasses – the local prostitutes whose tariffs reflected the price of a few cans of Carlsberg Special Brew and a packet of fags. I smiled briefly and nodded my head in acknowledgement. I wasn't interested in becoming friends with anyone in here.

'Have you got any swag, lad? Any bobby? I'm fucking rattling here, kidder,' Yozza said, whispering out the side of his mouth. His eyes were darting around the room, suspicious that someone might be listening.

'Piss off now. I'm here to get my shit together. It's a fucking detox not a retox,' I said, snarling. 'Go on, piss off before I drop you.'

First he looked shocked then hurt by my outburst. He opened his yellow-toothed mouth to say something but decided against it before skulking off to the garden where he stood talking animatedly with the two girls. After a couple of moments of Yozza's arm waving and head shaking, the two girls stared hard in my direction while he simply looked bemused. I fixed them with my most baleful glare, holding eye contact until they all had the courtesy to turn away. I was already fuming. Some fucking introduction to detox! I wanted to get through this the best way I could, no problems, no conflict, and with as little pain as possible, But already I was having to deal with all sorts of grief.

I was shown to a room that was pretty basic but better than nothing – I've been in far worse places, I reminded myself – and was told the doctor would see me shortly, so I unpacked, sat on the bed and stared out of the window, watching the squirrels clambering up and down a majestic oak tree on a cold October morning.

The doctor asked me how much I was using on top of my prescription. Why I lied I don't know but I told him only about £10 a day depending on what money I could beg, borrow or steal to fund my habit. I was using way more than that but feared being honest would affect my detox programme. He planned to reduce me from 80 ml by 5 ml a day, then prescribe me some sleepers combined with lofexidine, a medication that would help with the aches and pains.

'How are you feeling in general, Mr Moore?' he asked as he made notes of my answers.

Well, I wasn't feeling on good form and told him so. He told me I was probably depressed and that he would prescribe anti-depressants. Depressed? Was he serious? I was fucking rattling, that was the problem. I was dreading whatever was ahead of me: the fear of withdrawal usually had me in crisis and giving up before I had really begun, but this time I was determined to stop killing myself on a daily basis.

Yozza wasn't my cup of tea; he was a slippery animal, always up to no good, swapping medications and doing his best to sabotage his own and everybody else's treatment. I kept my distance and pretty quickly found myself feeling isolated. What mattered was my personal recovery. I remembered what a therapist had once told me in a group: if you looked to your left and then to your right you would see that one out of three of you was going to die of this illness called addiction, one had a very slim percentage of finding recovery and one would suffer in addiction for many years. *Fuck that*, I thought, *I'm not turning left or right, I'm determined to take the recovery route, no matter how narrow or bumpy it's going to be.*

Throughout the day we would have discussion groups and talks – all aimed at helping us come to terms and deal with our addiction. Of course, delivering a meaningful discussion topic to a motley mix of habitual addicts of mind-altering substances was challenging for the therapist to say the least. Most of the participants' brains were so scrambled from years of abuse we could have been discussing tropical fish in recovery for all we cared. Looking around, I felt I could have been on the film set of *Pirates of the Caribbean*. Some of my neighbours looked so rough they made Johnny Depp's Captain Jack Sparrow look like a model of clean living and abstinence.

In the first session, I studied my new group and listened carefully as the facilitator asked each of us to introduce ourselves: there were at least eight of us in the morning process group and these were the ones who could be bothered to engage, to drag themselves out of bed. We sat in a loose circle while Laura, the head therapist, encouraged us to participate.

An older guy in his sixties with a bulbous red nose introduced himself to the group first.

'Hi evvybody, my name is Witchie. I'm from Wock Felly in the Willal and my pwoblem is alcohol,' he slurred with a definite defect in his ability to pronounce the letter R.

There was a sudden outburst of laughter from Yozza. 'Witchie? Wock Felly? What the fuck are you saying, old timer?' he taunted.

'I'm solly but this is how I speak. There's no need to be abusive,' Ritchie said.

Laura intervened and warned the group about 'isms' while looking sternly at Yozza, who didn't seem at all interested in what she or anyone else had to say.

'How are you feeling, Ritchie?' Laura asked.

'I'm feeling tellable. Absolutely wough,' he replied, wiping away the solitary tear that rolled gently down the side of his face.

We left Ritchie sniffling as we moved on to the next person: a young guy in his early twenties who wore thick-rimmed glasses and had a little Hitler-style moustache. He looked odd and had a nervous twitch of some sort as his head was continuously bobbing forward as if he was impersonating a chicken.

'I'm Brandon, fuck, fuck, fuck, FUCK!' he screamed at the top of his lungs, causing everyone in the group to jump and then start sniggering, including myself. 'I've got a problem with legal highs, TWAT HOOKS, fuck, fuck, fuck and fuck him in the arse,' he said, quickly covering his mouth and apologising profusely.

Yozza just shook his head and mimed the crazy sign with his finger. I doubt he realised that young Brandon suffered with Tourette's and labelled everyone with a disability as being crazy. I strongly disliked Yozza already and was beginning to hate him and everything about his cocky, disdainful attitude.

A few girls in the group introduced themselves and one in particular, called Molly, a pretty thing who had let herself go and looked to be in her early thirties, had had it rough. She spoke about having a wonderful job as a nurse and how she began to take medication to deal with the pressures of work, especially after having a newborn baby to cope with as well. She told us about stealing patients' medication as her addiction progressed; how she got caught by her manager and lost her job; how her relationship ended and that led to social services getting involved after she began neglecting her daughter, who was also called Molly. She told us how her child was taken from her and how, suddenly, she found herself living on the streets, selling her body and begging for money to fund her ever-growing habit. She was depressed and desperate to get clean and stay clean. She cried in obvious agony as she shared her story with the group, and I felt truly sorry for her. Silently, I hoped she would succeed in her recovery.

Then it was my turn. I didn't have much to say. I knew why I was here, the shit I'd been through needed dealing with, especially the trauma I had endured growing up in an alcoholic household with a violent father, but I felt this group setting wasn't the best place to share that stuff, so I remained largely silent and kept it brief. I told them my name and said I was feeling confident and left it at that. I didn't want to talk about the nightmares that would wake me up in the early hours of the morning screaming, drenched in sweat. The fear I had for my father remained with me throughout my adult life and I realised that the copious amounts of drugs I took could not block out those memories. It just became worse as my drug use increased. I knew this was something I needed to deal with but who could I trust? I decided to bide my time and observe the landscape within the detox.

Yozza talked constantly about himself, his drug use and the big jobs he'd done over the years. His tales became wilder as he ranted on. I was bored and frankly lost interest the minute he opened his mouth. I knew enough to know that he was lost like the rest of us and that he probably wouldn't make it with the 'Big I am' attitude he had on permanent display. Some of us need to pretend we are someone else, to feel important or attach ourselves to someone to feel like a somebody. None of us wants to admit to ourselves that we are nobodies.

As the group came to a conclusion, Laura glanced over at me with a knowing look on her face. She smiled as I caught her eye; it was a smile that said you're going to be OK, just hang in there.

As evenings and free time came, co-dependants would cuddle up together on the sofas – poor souls looking for compassion and love, but in all the wrong places. I would smile wryly to myself as I sat on my own in a discrete corner with a jotter pad, writing down my experiences, hopes and dreams for the future. Being honest with myself and committing my feelings to words was the catharsis I needed to have any chance of success in beating my own demons.

Alf, the manager of the Kevin White Unit, a Mr Magoo lookalike with milk-bottle glasses, called me into his office one day to give me a bollocking. Apparently, anything with recording capabilities such as my MP3 player were on the banned list. I'd sneaked one in and it had 'come to his attention'. This digression from the rules was in itself enough to get me thrown out. That bemused me. I'd been used to prison regimes where smuggling stuff in got you thrown into solitary in the 'block', not thrown out on to the street! The paranoia was setting in. How did Mr Magoo know about my MP3? Who had grassed me up? Withdrawal from heroin, especially an on-off couple of decades' habit like mine, can play tricks with your sanity.

I got into a routine of hiding my MP3 player down the side of the sofa in the evenings with the record button on. As my fellow addicts huddled up on the other couches to gossip and plot their next illicit fix, the microphone picked up their conspiring. One of them was calling me a grass! I recognised the voice immediately – it was Yozza.

I listened to the playback in my room with growing anger and a sense of injustice boiling up inside me. What was wrong with these people? Because I didn't conform to their expectations, didn't look for ways to sabotage my own battle to get off drugs, didn't spend my evenings in the gossiping circle, how did that warrant being called a grass? He had to be jealous. There was no way I was being labelled a grass by anyone.

Five in the morning, stressed and unable to sleep, I crept down the passageway to my accuser's door, ready to confront him with the recorded evidence in hand. I was wired up to go toe-to-toe, to make him painfully aware of his own shortcomings. Of course, being confronted by me, my fists and their reputation at five in the morning wasn't going to be a pleasant prospect and he remained firmly behind the locked door. Fortunately, for me even more than for him, I gave up and went back to my room to calm down. Breakfast time and I was back in front of Mr Magoo for another bollocking. Irony of irony, I had been grassed up for threatening behaviour. Even Mr Magoo saw the funny side of things.

I was down to a daily 5 ml of methadone, the heroin substitute. Crashing down from an 80-ml daily habit was a pretty fast detox: my legs were aching and I struggled to sleep; my body was on fire with the pain of withdrawal, which had me jumping in and out of a cold bath at least five times a night. I would stalk the corridors and go out into the garden for some fresh air; anything to distract me from the thoughts of picking up drugs or making a run for it. I sang to myself as I paced up and down my room with the harsh early morning light stabbing my eyes:

> At two o'clock in the morning
> they'd emptied out the jug,
> Doyle lifted the icebox lid

to see poor Paddy's mug.
They changed the clocks
so Mrs Murphy couldn't tell the time,
and at quarter after two,
we argued it was nine.

A guy called Dean had been off his methadone for about ten days and we chatted a lot, more to pass the time than anything else really. He was a big, sensitive guy with a bald head, soft features and a nervous twitch in his left eye.

'Billy, I've met this girl. She's the one – honest, mate, she is,' he said, waving his arms about excitedly. 'She's definitely the one, lad. She makes me feel alive.'

His new love was an Irish lass called Imelda. Sadly, she was just as fucked up as he was but, as they say, broken people attract broken people.

'Dean, you met her in the medication line. It's a fucking rehab. Get your shit together, it's toxic, mate,' I said, wanting him to see sense. He never did and a couple of days later they both left, hand in hand, neither completing their full detox. I heard through the grapevine a couple of months later that Dean got arrested for robbery shortly after leaving detox and Imelda fell pregnant. The child was immediately taken off her. So much for rehab romances.

This was life or death to the likes of us; we don't get any second chances. I tried to share some of my experience about recovery with a few of the other lunatics around me, and I felt the need to encourage others to discover that there was a life beyond all the misery and suffering that had brought us here in the first place. I didn't want to see Dean or anyone else die out there in the grip of active addiction, but first things first: I needed to get my own shit together and get through this horrendous detox. I finally got my first day clean:

methadone free, my body felt weak but my will was strong. It wasn't easy, but I pushed through the hours one at a time, sometimes having to push through the minutes the same way.

To be honest, the daily group sessions didn't seem to help me. I had so much I wanted to talk about but didn't, couldn't, feel comfortable sharing it with my peers. I passed by Laura's office one morning, hoping she would emerge and ask me how I was feeling. For unknown reasons, I could never be the one to initiate the conversation that was needed.

'Billy, would you come in here for a moment?' I heard as I walked past her office. It was Laura and she wanted to speak with me.

'Yes, is everything OK?' Ever suspicious of anyone in authority.

'Yes, everything's fine. I'd just like to know how you're getting on. Please take a seat.' She gestured to the only other chair available in her tiny, cramped office. I sat with my hands under my bum feeling like a small boy in the headmaster's office. And I didn't say a word.

'I've noticed you've been attending the daily process groups but have yet to talk about why you're here,' she said, with a concerned look on her face. 'Is there anything you want to tell me? This is a safe place to share what's bothering you. No one here is going to pass judgement,' she added kindly.

I looked away as I felt myself welling up. The drugs by now were well and truly out of my system and I was overwhelmed with feelings that I couldn't identify or placate. Laura placed her warm, caring hand on top of mine.

'It's OK,' she said gently. 'You're safe here.'

I cried openly as I spoke about the abuse my father had subjected me to. Laura handed me a tissue and listened to me talk for what seemed like hours. It was like the scab of an old wound being peeled away to reveal the new, healed skin beneath, and by the time I finished there were no more tears. All the while Laura remained silent, allowing me to begin the journey of freeing myself of all the guilt and shame that didn't and shouldn't belong to me.

I thanked her and left her office feeling lighter in spirit and somehow relieved. Over the next couple of weeks Laura spoke with me on more than half-a-dozen occasions and each time I left her cramped office I felt altogether stronger and more hopeful about my future. She was amazing and helped me massively in my early recovery.

A beautiful Russian lap dancer called Mishka walked through the doors of the Kevin White one day. With typically high Slavic cheekbones, cascading blonde hair and legs that went on for ever, she looked totally out of place but obviously had a problem with something. All the lads were drooling over her, falling over each other to help carry her bags. Yozza moved in fast, chatting her up in a cringeworthy way. I don't know how he managed it, but he seemed to have pulled; they became inseparable over the next couple of days, causing a lot of jealousy among some of the other guys and girls.

I was glad that they were distracted by the legs of Leningrad; at least it stopped them from gossiping about me. I had seen enough and realised my best chance of recovery was to stay out of everyone's way. The only thing I was going to learn from these guys was what they didn't have much of – patience and tolerance. They were something I would definitely need in the future.

'What's happening, Witchie?' Yozza shouted from the sofa one evening while cuddled up to Mishka. They were both laughing at poor Ritchie. I just sat and listened, not wanting to get involved. My problem has always been wanting to fight the underdog's battles. I hated bullies after being bullied myself as a child at home and at school.

'Vitchie,' Mishka said slowly in her Russian accent, mimicking Yozza and giggling like a naughty schoolgirl. *How the fuck can she take*

44

the piss out of anyone with the clothes she's wearing? I thought. Mrs Molotov sitting there like a bad scruff in her fake, pasty Ugg boots and dirty yellow leggings with a cheap purple hoodie. Don't get me started on Yozza. Who the fuck he thought he was I didn't know. He sat there in a pair of shorts and flip-flops with the world's worst toenails, the type that could rip open safes, and to top it off he wore a dirty, sweat-stained gym vest that was way too big for him. Being judgemental was a great way to escape the madness of this asylum.

'Stop this now. I'm not here to be mocked by anyone,' Ritchie retaliated as he sat at the table, building something architectural out of matchsticks. What he was making I had no idea, probably a ladder for all I cared. I just carried on watching cartoon-life happening all around me.

'Shut up, bellwhiff. You remind me of Woger from *The Life of Brian*. Have you ever seen that, Witchie?' Yozza laughed loudly, some of the other clientele in the detox joining in and taunting old Ritchie. He had become a routine source of amusement during evening free time.

Brandon was doing his chicken impersonation with his little Hitler moustache, constantly shouting at the top of his voice the most vulgar profanities you could imagine. 'Big wanks . . . fat titties . . . cunt, cunt, cunt.' The whole unit was fucked up with people who were here because they weren't all there.

My detox was coming to an end. I was four days clean and felt terrible. There was no aftercare and nothing in place for my ongoing treatment in the community; my only hope was the recovery meetings and I knew I had to jump right into the middle of the boat, otherwise I'd sink back into the abyss of addiction.

Everybody received a certificate congratulating them on a success-ful detox. Those who had stayed the duration would leave them on the pool table for everyone to sign and write farewell messages.

I couldn't be bothered with people writing bullshit about what a great guy they thought I was and how sad they were going to be to see me leave, especially as some hated the sight of me. The most common comment was the title lyric of 'Shine on You Crazy Diamond'. Well, I'm no expert on 1960s rock but I seem to remember reading that Pink Floyd were stoned when they wrote that song about the mental decline of Syd Barrett – hardly a fitting epitaph for someone departing a drugs detox.

I didn't want to go with the flow, I wanted to swim upstream and stand out from the rest. Not everyone in there was my cup of tea – they would be happy to see you fail. I'd rather eat crumbs with bums than steaks with snakes. My journey was one I would have to travel alone. I left the detox with a meetings list from big Eddie, a volunteer worker, and ventured out into the city with huge plans of becoming a productive member of society. Maybe even write a book and fall in love.

Chapter 5
Toxic

Love comforeth like sunshine after rain,
But Lust's effect is tempest after sun.
Love's gentle spring doth always fresh remain;
Lust's winter comes ere summer half be done.
Love surfeits not, Lust like a glutton dies;
Love is all truth, Lust full of forged lies.

Venus and Adonis, William Shakespeare

I WAS never good at relationships. I was a bad picker when it came to choosing a good woman, or any woman for that matter. If you told me you would totally ruin my life and make me miserable for years to come, then I'd probably move in with you right away.

For many years I was in a toxic relationship with a lady called Heroin. She abused me, but not at first. In the beginning she seduced me, she was kind to me, she treated me like I was someone special. It was love. We escaped together and went to some far-out places. The relationship blossomed but within months she changed. She became painful to be around, keeping me awake at nights, watching me shiver, splutter and vomit. The gentle warmth she had given me was now gone. She belittled me and put me down; she sold all my property; she stole my self-esteem; destroyed my self-worth and robbed me blind. I couldn't let go. I needed her and she needed me. It was just the two of us and we were in it together.

'You will never leave me,' Lady Heroin would whisper in my ear. 'You need me. I will never let you go.'

She stole my heart, my life, my family and then, in the end, took me to prison. I tried to end our relationship and refuse her advances . . . but even in prison she never left me. The nights were the worst. She would creep into my cell and whisper, 'Just one more.' It was never just one more. She would chain herself to my soul and break me at every opportunity. Enough was enough, the relationship had to end. We had been together for almost fifteen years. The cell was dark and she stood alone in the corner becoming weaker each time I screamed 'No.' I fought her, no longer would I allow her to defeat me . . .

I became free, but she would stalk me for years to come. Always ready to pounce at any sign of weakness on my part. These were the type of women I met.

I was only six months clean when I met a girl with a similar background to me. She was 'the one'! The truth was, every woman I had ever met was 'the one' but just maybe this one was different. Her name was Samantha, and she lived in Runcorn, not far from Liverpool. I was emotionally underdeveloped and poorly equipped with the skills to deal with intimacy. I was still struggling and wanted to be loved by anyone who would have me; to be needed and not feel used or abandoned. My friends tried to warn me of the dangers of meeting someone who was as damaged as I was, but I wouldn't listen to anyone. Not even my sponsor and mentor, Ash. He was a man of vast experience in relationships and not even he could get through to me. I was blind and my judgement was clouded with fantasies of love. He told me unequivocally how it was from his perspective:

'If you're man enough to get into a relationship, you're man enough to deal with the feelings.'

These were his words of wisdom; his attitude was to get on your knees and pray when the shit hits the fan. Only I wasn't a man. Physically, I looked like a man but internally I was still a boy who found growing up and taking responsibility frightening. Despite my flirtations with the 'evils of heroin', I remained an atheist and found it difficult to believe in any kind of religion, so getting on my knees was out of the question. *It is love*, I told myself. It had to be because the sex was great and isn't that what made a loving relationship work? I sat in the meetings and became closed-minded to other people sharing their terrible experiences with women. I was choosing denial rather than a more painful reality.

One guy shared his resentment in a meeting about his recent escapade with a woman he had met that had ended badly. 'They're nuts, all of them. Would you shop in the dented-can aisle of the local supermarket or go on a date with a girl from a mental asylum? I didn't use the steps and nuts means, "Not Using The Steps": that's what happens when you don't work a programme, you end up in fucked-up relationships with crazy ladies.'

However, my relationship was different. This was love after all! At times, relationships are a struggle – everyone knows that. Only deep down I *knew* it was one-sided. I suffered with dependency and became very needy and this became apparent to my family and friends. Samantha became my higher power and I would live for the weekend in total anxiety, wondering if she would want to see me. I tried my best to keep busy and continued writing about my patterns of behaviour. Maybe if I wrote about how I felt, I could understand how I ticked. Abandoning myself, feeling rejected by others and most of the time just feeling used. I didn't value anything about who I was and suffered with constant low self-esteem. To be alone frightened me, and it became my biggest fear – loneliness. I realised as time went on that I felt lonely next to the woman I believed I loved.

I tried desperately to make things work with Samantha, even planning to have children. Maybe that was what I was missing? The opportunity to be a loving father to my own child. She became pregnant and the excitement was indescribable. We told our families and my mother was utterly joyful and immediately began to knit shawls and search the internet for baby products; having raised six kids, my mother was endearingly maternal.

Then, out of the blue one evening, Samantha announced that she didn't think it was a good idea to go ahead with the pregnancy. Shocked, hurt and deeply confused by what I'd just heard, I broke down and begged her to reconsider. She became angry and told me to leave. I went back to my own apartment, struggling with my own thoughts. I was trying to work out what had gone wrong. Everything seemed fine the day before. Had someone said something? What had she heard? Why the sudden change of mind? I had a 'one year clean' birthday coming up in a few days and despite my non-belief prayed to God to help me through the anguish. I held on for dear life, not wanting to use, but these inexorable feelings were almost impossible to bear. I also knew that picking up drugs wasn't the answer and maybe she'd change her mind. I did the next best thing and called a friend who came over and sat with me through my troubled times. I didn't use drugs that day to change the way I was feeling.

Sitting in a meeting, one year clean should have been a time for celebration but for me it was a time of desperation. I couldn't concentrate on anything; my mind was preoccupied with thoughts of dread. I hadn't heard from Samantha since our last conversation and I had a powerful need to know. It was torture and the silent treatment was killing me. During the meeting interval, I sent her a text, pleading with her to give me an answer and to stop this torment, to have some compassion. I looked at my phone hoping for an instant reply, but there was nothing. What had I done to deserve this? Getting the silent treatment was a form of control and abuse. I tried to focus on the guy who was sharing his experience in recovery and took a few deep breaths, closed my eyes and hoped I could hear a message of hope instead of the noise that was going on in my mind.

Ping . . . *Ping* . . . Two messages came in quick succession. My feelings shifted and, feeling a little hope, I took a deep breath and looked down at the screen. The messages were from my Samantha and simply read that she was terminating the pregnancy and ending our relationship. My whole world was tumbling down around me. Panic-stricken, I left the meeting without even collecting my twelve-month key tag, my badge of honour for not using drugs for a whole year.

I still didn't use this as an excuse to pick up drugs; I gritted my teeth and curled up in a ball, crying almost uncontrollably for the next few days. Eventually I went to visit my sister Lisa. I needed to get out of my apartment before I lost my mind and I feared relapsing. I would keep repeating to myself the mantra, 'No matter what, you don't have to use.' I would also say the 'Serenity Prayer' often used by Alcoholics and Narcotics Anonymous, asking for courage, anything to get me through the pain that had engulfed my whole being, because I knew for me to use would lead to terrible consequences.

My father, Tony, lived around the corner from my sister and would visit regularly. He was there when I arrived. 'Hello son, you OK?' he asked.

'Hmm, yeah, I'm OK. How have you been?' I asked.

He coughed violently and spluttered, 'I'm all right,' and then he looked at me and said, 'If you need anything, I'm here for you. I heard what happened and I think she's really selfish . . . I do love you, son. You can always talk to me.'

It was nice to hear those words from him. I knew he was trying his best to make up for the years we'd lost due to his alcoholism and violence and, no matter what, he was still my father. He coughed again, made a roll-up and bade farewell to me and his daughter.

I'd decided I had to deal with the fears I had around my dad not long after leaving detox. I'd heard from my mother that my father was living in a hostel south of the city. He had become a heavy street drinker and resorted to selling the *Big Issue* not long after my mother kicked him out of our home. It was a frosty day in mid-January when I ventured out and headed to the hostel. I was raw, angry, but afraid at the same time. I went along with my five-year-old niece Megan, holding tightly on to her hand as we walked together.

The hostel was a rundown building with a big green door. No one manned the front desk and only the sound of a tinny radio from an upper level playing eighties rock music suggested the building was occupied. Paint was peeling off the walls and a thick cloud of cigarette smoke gave the atmosphere a foggy look. You could immediately tell that it was a rough place. I took along Megan because she had visited before with her mum and knew exactly what room her grandad, my father, was in.

It had been almost ten years since I had last seen him, and our conversations back then had been brief or non-existent. Standing outside his door, I took a deep breath, raised my hand to knock then paused, unsure of whether I could go through with it. What was I going to say him anyway? I had many questions and a tank full of blame, but I was lacking in both confidence and courage. Before I knew it, Megan was knocking on the door and shouting for her grandad to answer.

'It's open,' a gravelly, unwell voice shouted back.

Slowly, I inched forward, the door creaking loudly on long-unoiled hinges as I pushed at it. There, sitting on a stool, was my dad, wearing a flat cap with stray bits of straggly grey hair protruding from the sides.

'Hello Dad, how are you? It's been a while,' I said, feeling like the little boy of many years ago and not the man I was today. It was strange how he made me feel every time I was around him . . . intimidated. I glanced at him. He looked old and frail, not at all like the huge man I remembered.

Something happened next that made me shudder: my father looked up at me and our eyes locked. In that moment, I saw all of his guilt and shame. His bloodshot and yellowing eyes were full of sadness and pain. He was hurting badly. I was transfixed and couldn't look away; my feelings were all over the place and I began to well up but quickly swallowed it down. We hadn't been allowed to express any emotions when growing up and certainly never allowed to cry. My father looked away and his voice faltered for a moment.

'It is good to see you, son,' he said simply.

Little more was said; my visit lasted little more than ten minutes. I held Megan's hand tightly as we walked out into the bitter cold, the tears beginning to sting my eyes. It was the precise moment I forgave my father for everything he had put us through over the years. Megan squeezed my hand even tighter, looked up at me and, with the magical inner-knowledge children seem to possess, told me everything was going to be OK. The sun was shining for me on that frosty day and a weight had been removed from my shoulders and my heart. It was time to move on and even build a relationship with my father again.

I still loved Samantha, even though she'd broken my heart by terminating the pregnancy. The dependant in me wouldn't let go and after a few weeks she got back in touch suggesting we meet for coffee. Of course I would. I was lonely. It was a recipe for disaster.

My head was a mess; I couldn't cope with all this drama again. Any trust I had in her was lost and why I kept going back to her confused me. We were never going to be a family and this relationship was really screwing me up. Not long later, I was sat on the train heading back from Runcorn to Liverpool after being kicked out of Samantha's home for using colourful language; it was a pattern that would happen quite regularly and for some reason I would always blame myself. This time it was justified, believe me. I was fed up of being controlled by a passive aggressive.

Unbelievably, the latest argument was over chocolate biscuits. I would often wake during the night and would pop downstairs for a snack. It pissed Samantha off, or so she told me. This particular evening, I had slipped out of bed as quietly as a member of the special forces while she slept on. I opened the biscuit tin and helped myself to three chocolate digestives. The next day Samantha confronted me over the crime.

'Did you eat any biscuits last night?' she demanded, eyeing me up and down suspiciously.

'Who me? No, of course not,' I said, immediately feeling a deep sense of shame.

'Someone did,' she snapped.

'How do you know?' I asked, feigning ignorance.

Her young son (from a previous relationship) stood next to her with his hands planted on his more than ample hips, looking at me with the contempt only the young can muster. I felt as if I was on trial or being interrogated by the Kray twins in a single-light-bulbed basement.

'Because. I. Counted. Them,' Samantha said, waving the tin with the flourish of a top QC at the Old Bailey.

'What the fuck! Why would you count them? OK, I had a biscuit. Big fucking deal,' I said, reacting badly to the theatrical accusation.

'Get out of my house now!' she screamed, pointing to the door.

'Are you serious? How am I going to get home? You live in the sticks,' I said, fuming at her ridiculous outburst over a 38p packet of biscuits. Who the fuck counts biscuits before going to bed anyway?

'If you don't go now, I'll call the police,' she said. Her face was weirdly contorted with a look of sheer hatred.

'I'm going nowhere. I can't even get a bus home. You are not exiling me here in *Deep Space Nine*,' I said, convinced she would calm down and see sense. Unfortunately, she didn't. The police came and I left, but they were kind enough to drop me off at the train station.

Of all the people I had to bump into while sitting on the train, feeling both angry and sorry for myself, was Purple Aki. Purple Aki was a known sexual predator who had a history of stalking rugby teams and feeling muscles. My first experience of meeting him was when I was sixteen years old. He was behind me, whistling a tune. He smiled and asked me if I'd just been the gym. I told him I had. He then asked me how big my muscles were. I told him I wasn't sure, so he asked me to tense, which I did and then he felt them. I thought nothing of it until he asked if I knew which the biggest muscle in the body was. I wasn't sure but said it was the back. He told me it wasn't, it was the leg . . . whereupon he asked me to tense mine. I soon realised who he was: the notorious Aki who got a kick out of feeling muscles. He was the bogeyman, a myth, a horror story your parents would tell you about when you were growing up. Before he had the chance to grab my leg, I made my excuses and started to jog home with Aki running easily alongside me, all the while asking me where I was going. Now I sprinted full pelt and made it to my front door and flew through it with Aki close on my heels. I slammed the door shut behind me, breathing heavily, while Aki remained on the step banging the letterbox.

My mother wanted to know what was going on. I quickly told her who and what Aki was. She knew of him, of course, and told me to go upstairs while she dealt with it. I heard raised voices, the threat of police and then a door slam shut. My mother had chased him away from our home. He never came back, but he would chase me every time he saw me, scaring the living daylights out of me.

Now, here I was sitting opposite the man on a train, pouring out my heart and on the receiving end of relationship guidance from him! In a funny and ironic way, I liked him and he held no fear for me any more. He was a lot older and had served a lot of time in prison for his outlandish behaviour, which was his form of addiction. He told me what everyone else had told me before – to stop selling myself short and to stop settling for crumbs. This was from Aki, who had been dangerous in his day. Rumour had it that six IRA terrorists had once followed him into the toilets in Strangeways prison to deal with him. There had been loud thumps and bangs, and then Aki had appeared alone, shaking his hands after dismantling the six guys. So, according to Aki, it was inevitable my relationship would end.

The hold this woman had over me was overpowering. I was becoming really unhappy but didn't know how to let go. It was just a game we played: an on-off, yo-yo relationship, and there was little doubt I'd go back to her soon enough. It was insanely toxic.

Chapter 6

Hurricane

Wise men ne'er sit and wail their loss but cheerily seek how to redress their harms.

Henry VI, Part 3 Act 5, Scene 4,
William Shakespeare

HOPE Street, Liverpool. The Anglican Cathedral at one end dominates the city skyline while at the other end its more modern Catholic rival, 'Paddy's Wigwam' to the locals, vies for attention. I'd hopped off the bus at one end of the street and was making my way to the drug service where I volunteered in nearby Rodney Street. Passing bars, restaurants, boutiques and passageway doors leading to beauty salons and dental services, I noticed a brass plaque beside one particular nondescript red door. 'Hurricane Films' was etched into polished brass next to a doorbell inviting callers to ring it. I hesitated for a moment, then made the decision to push the button. A tinny voice answered.

'Hurricane Films. Nicole speaking.'

As I leaned in to reply, the door buzzed and clicked open. By the time I reached the office at the top of the stairs, I was huffing and puffing – blowing hard from the climb. Nicole was alone in the small office. She was an attractive lady with dark eyes and olive skin and possibly Middle Eastern features. She eyed me with some suspicion and, considering my less-than-smart appearance, was evidently apprehensive. I looked around the office, crowded with files.

'Can I speak to the manager, please? I have something I hope he'll be interested in,' I said, patting the plastic shopping bag I was clutching.

'Er, no one's here today, they'll be back tomorrow,' she told me. I got the hint that I was being dismissed, nodded and left.

I rang the bell again the next day but the door wasn't buzzed open this time. The same voice spoke to me through the intercom, politely telling me the managers were not in again and she wasn't sure when they would be back. On the third day I was back again, ringing the bell. Nicole came down this time to meet me and kept me firmly on the doorstep. I explained I had written a book and wanted to hand it to the manager to read. She looked at me, some of her apprehension and resistance beginning to fade and a glimmer of an amused smile flitting across her mouth.

'If you hand it to me, I'll make sure they get it,' she promised.

I was in two minds what to do because this was my personal copy and the only one I owned. Derek, my Southeast Asian publisher, had sent it to me. Now it was my turn to be apprehensive as I handed over the dog-eared and tatty copy of *A Prayer Before Dawn*.

'Are you sure? Don't you need my details?' I asked Nicole.

'Of course. Your email and phone number should be enough. You should hear back in about twelve weeks,' she told me.

I reluctantly handed over my details and the precious book as she closed the door. *We'll see*, I thought to myself.

The months passed and I was on the bus one day feeling typically despondent at the direction my relationship was heading. The termination of the pregnancy had affected me but still, somehow, I had misguided feelings of love for Samantha even though, deep down, I recognised the relationship was far from good for me. I couldn't let go and hoped things between us would magically improve. It was based on lust not love; that was the confusion. Dark clouds of depression had formed above my head and followed me around constantly; was it ever going to get any better? My mobile rang, startling me and pulling me back into the present, away from my doleful reverie.

'Hey Billy, its Nicole from Hurricane. How are you today?'

Nicole? Hurricane? Moments passed before it finally registered. Hurricane Films. Wow, had it been three months already?

'Hiya, fine thanks,' I stammered, surprised but then feeling both anxious and a little excited.

'Well, Roy and Sol, my managers, have read your manuscript and would like a meeting with you as soon as possible. They're delighted with your story and would like to know when you can come in for a chat.'

'I'm free now,' I said, kicking myself for sounding too eager and even desperate.

'OK, tomorrow afternoon, around two o'clock at the office. See you then. Bye now.' She ended the call and was gone.

I couldn't believe it! Someone was interested in making a documentary about my life. I called my mum immediately, who was overjoyed and excited. Finally, someone liked my story.

The next afternoon I was back in Hope Street, taking a deep breath at the door of Hurricane Films. I'd enjoyed some success as my book had been published in Thailand and could be found on the shelves of bookstores in Southeast Asia, so I should have been feeling reasonably confident, but I wasn't. I was nervous as hell. A documentary about my book maybe? Wow. I didn't know what to expect. Nicole ushered me in and introduced me to Roy Boulter and Sol Papadopoulos – the owners of Hurricane Films.

Both were from Liverpool, well at least Roy was. Sol sounded like a posh scouser. We sat around a small table. In front of Roy was my dog-eared book looking even more beaten up. Notebook in hand and pen at the ready, he flattered me with his opening remarks.

'OK, Billy, it's nice to meet you, and what a fantastic story. We gave this book to all our readers and for the first time in the ten years we have been in business, every one of them put their hand up and said that this was a story worth pursuing.'

'OK, that sounds good,' I said, doing my best to hide my excitement and play it cool. It was sounding promising for that documentary . . .

'Let's get straight to the point,' said Sol. 'We want to make a feature film about your story.'

'What!? A feature film!' I exclaimed, completely blown away. They could all see how surprised I was.

'Yes, a movie,' Roy said, his smile sharing my delight.

I left Roy and Sol's office a couple of hours later still in shock but full of hope and excited at the prospect of my book becoming a movie. I really couldn't believe my luck; you couldn't write this. I told anyone and everyone who would listen and shared it proudly on all social media sites. I constantly went on about it and probably annoyed an awful lot of people. Some listened with a sympathetic ear, others looked and reacted like I had mental health problems, but I didn't care because I knew the truth. I was like a small child locked in a sweet shop, an excitable puppy craving attention. I just wanted everyone to share in my good news.

People with big egos usually suffer with hidden low self-esteem (imposter syndrome), and this was something I would painfully learn as time went on. I didn't have many followers on social media at the time but that soon changed. However, my mum was and still is my Number One fan and was immensely proud, and it filled my heart with joy to see her so happy. It was a delight to the soul.

It gave my life a new purpose. All I wanted to do was tell my story and maybe inspire someone to change their lives for the better; it was a story of hope and redemption in the most unlikely of places.

During my meeting with Roy I'd learned that he had been in a band called The Farm that had the nineties hit 'All Together Now'. The tune played over in my head as I made my way home. Perhaps my newfound success would be the kickstart my relationship with Samantha needed. How wrong could I be. Nothing I learned outside of me could fix an internal problem.

In the following weeks, with a new zest and passion, I found myself an Irish-based English language publisher, after being encouraged to do so by Derek, who had first brought my book to market in South-East Asia. I'd sent loads of letters and received my fair share of refusals but never gave up and in doing so one letter with a positive reply landed on my doormat: it was an offer to publish here in the UK and Ireland. Maverick House of Dublin were ready to deal! A new jacket for the book was produced. Gone was the old prison ID front cover of me and in its place the picture of a hand hanging out of a cell.

Nick Saltrese had been hired to write the film script. The first thing I noticed about him was his height – he was at least six foot four with a bald head and a greying beard. Nick was a local lad in his late forties and had been a scriptwriter for TV programmes such as *The Bill* and *Brookside*, so a movie script was something new, but he was confident it could be done. We spent many mornings in the Café Tabac on Bold Street in Liverpool city centre. I would relive my journey repeatedly, paying a lot of attention to detail, while Nick wrote everything in his little notebook.

'How long will this take, Nick?' I asked, curious.

'It could be at least three years, Billy. It all depends on if we can sell the script. I've had a script in the making for almost ten years and it's still on the shelf,' he told me.

'As long as that . . . ?' I said, my enthusiasm waning as I sank back into my chair.

'Yeah, sorry mate. And you have to remember, it may never even make it to the screen in all honesty,' he said, crushing my hopes even more – as if I wasn't disappointed enough already. 'Don't worry, I'm sure it will do OK. It is a great story after all,' Nick added brightly, doing his best to reassure.

We spent a lot of time going over the script. I often struggled with the dialogue. The script didn't seem authentic. Although I knew that the movie would only be based on my life story and the scriptwriters would have to interpret it for the screen, it was my story and I didn't want it to be so loosely based. I wanted it to be told as accurately as possible. My motive was to tell a story of a journey through addiction, the fight for redemption and the desperation and loneliness I felt on that journey. I would speak with Roy and Sol at least once a week, email my thoughts on the script to everyone and press to keep the script as authentic as possible. I also had a financial goal; I could maybe make a living here. While all this was going on, I was unemployed. Also, having been through some serious shit in my life, I wanted to use my time for good and give something back to my community. In between movie talk I would volunteer for a charity called 'Genie in the Gutter', a place for people suffering with drug and alcohol addiction that helps them to build a bridge to normal living.

One afternoon Roy phoned. They had a potential director – a guy from France called Jean-Stéphane Sauvaire. His last movie was about African boy soldiers in Liberia. It was called *Johnny Mad Dog* and the cast, far from being professional actors, were actually former boy soldiers. The film was different from anything I had ever seen before. A documentary-style arthouse film instead of a mainstream action movie. And I enjoyed it! Critically acclaimed, it had great scores on IMBD and Rotten Tomatoes – the top two movie websites that review and score every movie released internationally. So, we had a director! The next step was a lead actor, and then finance. It was really exciting being involved in the whole process. We would all go out for breakfast and I would be given progress updates. Roy and Sol would travel to film festivals all around the world pitching *A Prayer Before Dawn* or (*APBD* as it became known) to potential financiers. For the first time in a long, long time, I felt part of something good, positive and meaningful.

I kept busy doing my voluntary work, helping out in all sorts of community services, learning new skills that would help me find future employment, anything other than criminality or drugs. My voluntary work saw me helping out with drug and alcohol services, the homeless, and anti-knife and gun crime campaigns throughout Merseyside for roughly eighteen months. I was ready for interviews for proper jobs. Well, I thought I was. My first job interview was a disaster and I didn't get the job. I went back for another interview for a more junior role and didn't get that either. I suppose a lifetime in and out of prison, the highlight being three years in jail in Thailand, didn't make for a very impressive CV.

I kept going, though, and put in an application for a post as a drug and alcohol support worker with a local charity. Drug abuse – no one could claim to have more experience than me. I got an interview on a Friday afternoon and was told I would hear on Monday if I'd been hired. I didn't hold out much hope but that Friday evening, sitting at home with a microwave meal for one and nothing stronger than a Diet Coke, my mobile rang. It was Mike, who had been on the interviewing panel. Was I sitting down? I'd got the job. 'Why wait all weekend to tell you?' he said.

For the first time in my life I had gained full-time honest proper employment. I was working directly with people in addiction. It kept me busy and fulfilled and I enjoyed my new role. As time went on, I developed a few friendships at my place of work, including with Mike. He was down to earth, what I would consider as one of the lads, and became a good friend. He helped me an awful lot during my time there and I will never forget what he did. The only problem with my new job was my line manager. He was a bully who would overwhelm me with work, setting difficult targets, and most of my time was spent pulling files from the storeroom.

Because I'd written a book people were interested, even intrigued, by my story and work colleagues would ask me how my book sales or the ongoing film project were getting on. This did not go down well with my manager, whose nose was well and truly put out of joint. Why? I really didn't know. I was hardly a famous author. I was asked, or more accurately forced, to send out a general email to all the staff with instructions not to ask me about my 'private affairs'.

Things got worse. One day I was called to the office by the area manager and warned about publishing anything on social media or in the press and magazines. I was more or less being told to get prior approval for anything to do with my private life. Of course, the rebellious streak in me prevailed. Maverick House, my publisher, had organised a book launch in the big and very prestigious Waterstones bookstore in Liverpool ONE, the shopping complex in the city. It was publicised as 'An evening with Billy Moore' and would promote the new edition of the book. The launch coincided nicely with the film project, which by now was gathering momentum.

I'd invited some friends and colleagues from work but didn't comply with the formal request to my work management. What possessed me to think I could get away with that I'll never know; the event was plastered all over Waterstones' window and every social media site possible. In the middle of the afternoon, I got the inevitable phone call from work on my mobile. I winced as Helen, my area manager, told me forthrightly that news of my event had 'come to her attention' and she wanted to know what on earth was going on. My breezy suggestion that I arrange some complimentary tickets for her and my line manager didn't go down too well. Sternly, I was told to report into the office the following morning.

Pissed off, I called Mike to protest but he told me not to worry and to get on with the launch. A good job he did, because it was a great evening and a real success. The bookstore was packed. Roy and Sol were there working their public relations charm and filming the whole event. I had to pinch myself just to make sure it was all real and not a dream. The bad dreams, the nightmare of prison in Thailand faded for a while as I began to look to the future of settling down, leading a normal life, maybe starting a family and using my story and past life to help others with their own demons.

Next day, I was in the office receiving a warning for holding an event in my own time without informing the powers that be. I bit my tongue and accepted my reprimand. My job was too important to me and I didn't want to lose it.

I was in work one day and I had received a few missed calls from my mother. It was unusual for her to call me during work hours so at the first opportunity I called her back.

'Hello. You OK, Mum?' I asked, concerned. I knew there was something wrong with her.

'Yeah, I'm fine, son. It's your dad. He's been rushed to hospital, and they think he's got cancer!' Although they had been separated for years they still had a close relationship and my poor mum was clearly distressed.

'Hmm. OK, Mum. Where is he and are you going to be OK?' I asked.

'He's in Whiston Hospital with our Kevin. I'm OK. I'm with our Lisa and Walla,' she told me between sobs.

Walla was my mum's husband and a good man who I respected. He treated my mum like a princess and brought out the best in her.

I was in shock over the news and struggled through the rest of the day. When I signed out, I phoned my friend John and shared the news with him. We met up and travelled to the hospital together. My father was in his bed, still wearing his hat. He looked terribly gaunt and grey. His weight had plummeted and I knew immediately it wasn't good. I didn't really know what to do. I tried to make him feel comfortable and paid for his TV viewing. All the while John sat quietly on one of the visitors' chairs. Him being there was a tower of strength. The doctors had yet to have all the results back but suspected cancer. We had no idea where it was but I assumed it was lung cancer due to his smoking habit. My father had been off the drink for over four years.

My father passed away on 19 December 2014 at 10.28 a.m. precisely, surrounded by his loving family. Our childhood memories of his drunkenness were a long time in the past. We held his hand as he took his final breath. The room went cold the moment he died. It was felt by everyone – his life force had moved on. My sister Lisa was screaming, tears rolling down her contorted face. 'Please don't go, Dad.' My brothers were also grief stricken. I had grieved every day he'd been in hospital and softly said, 'Let him go, let him sleep.' That evening I carried a message to the newcomers at one of the meetings I continued to attend. Current using wasn't a requirement.

Life went on. I told my mother one day that I intended to set up home with my girlfriend, Samantha. My mother, my friends and everyone who knew me were against it. My mate John wouldn't be drawn and steadfastly kept his opinions to himself. Later, I found out he was dead set against it. I, of course, knew best and moved in against everyone's wishes.

The relationship drifted on but inside a few months the fractures began to appear. I had the notion that a holiday break was what we needed to rekindle the spark. I booked us an all-inclusive deal in Sharm el-Sheikh in Egypt. On the first day Samantha went and sat in the blistering sun for hours covered in suntan oil, frying herself in 40 degrees heat. Suffering from the inevitable sunstroke, she eventually saw sense and staggered off to the showers to cool off. Feeling dizzy, she slipped over in the shower, splitting her head open and giving herself a black eye in the process.

Over the next five or six days of typical tourist pursuits, such as camel rides at the pyramids and a River Nile cruise, she looked like the loser in an unlicensed cage fight. Meanwhile I had to fend off both accusing looks from my fellow tourists and conspiratorial nudges and winks from unshaven waiters and camel-keepers convinced I'd given her a beating.

Samantha's twelve-year-old son, having never been further afield than Wales, refused to have anything to do with the food unless it was pizza, chicken nuggets or a burger – none of which tend to feature on North African menus. His constant whining and incessant demand for ice cream and cola, which would contribute to his already significant puppy fat, had me referring to him (behind his mother's back) as the Fat Controller.

The holiday was a disaster. The rekindling of the spark I had hoped for ignited an inferno of residual rage between us. Soon after our return from Egypt we acrimoniously split, leaving me alone in a too big, half-empty house. Actually, I wasn't completely alone. Her cat stayed. The cat was a black-and-white tom, fully intact and determined to go out on a nightly basis to prove his reproductive prowess and to scrap with each and every local rival. He would come in from his excursions demanding food while treating me with utter contempt. I hated that tomcat. He was called Rosie. Maybe that was his problem. Who in their right mind calls a tomcat Rosie? Rosie and I rattled around in the big house, tolerating each other with resignation and, as the months rolled by, I had to admit to myself I had, over the years, been forced to share with far less accommodating cellmates. So, in the end, I suppose we didn't get on too badly.

Every month the landlord would come around to collect his rent, always insistent on cash. And, as the list of outstanding repairs gradually grew, he would find an equally long list of excuses not to fix anything. The gas and electricity bills were included in the rent payments, a fair deal, I thought at first, until one evening the sparking from the hotwired electric meter nearly set the house on fire. I had to get that sorted but the landlord's excuses kept coming. I suppose it wasn't my best idea, but a few weeks before the Egypt holiday, I'd spent over £1,000 on decorating the house from top to bottom. Not wanting someone else to enjoy the benefits of my improvements and determined not to add credence to my mother and sister's 'I told you it was a bad idea' lectures on moving in with Samantha, I doggedly hung on to the tenancy of the big house. I liked its character, but it was expensive and now I was the only one paying the rent.

My mate Podge called me one day. He had a mate called Mark who was in need of somewhere to live. A teetotaller, working full time and well able to pay a share of rent . . . It was the proverbial no-brainer and with that Mark moved in. At last I was able to meet the month's rent without stressing about how I was going to manage to get through until next payday.

I worked hard at my job and I was even nominated for recovery worker of the year in 2015–16. I felt proud of what I had achieved, considering my past. I was eventually given a pay rise and could manage my bills a lot better, but the hangover of my recent failed relationship (and the way it ended) still tormented me. The lonely evenings at home and the uninvited fantasises I was having about meeting the 'one' caused me to act out and behave inappropriately. Everything was going well and my life was so full, so why did I feel so empty inside? This question I would ask myself had no answer. I talked to myself on a regular basis, positive pep talks about gratitude and what the future potentially had in store for me, but there was always that need for more. Nothing was ever enough.

Chapter 7

Paris

Oh! it offends me to the soul to hear a robust periwig-pated fellow tear
a passion to tatters, to very rags, to split the ears of the groundlings . . .

Hamlet Act 3, Scene 2,
William Shakespeare

CHARLIE Hunnam is the actor from England who played Jax in the American TV series *Sons of Anarchy* and was now lined up to play me in *A Prayer Before Dawn*. Jean-Stéphane, the French director, was on board and I was due to meet him for the first time in a couple of weeks and also be introduced to Rita Dagher − a producer from Paris. I was excited as it kept me busy and my mind occupied; it had only been a few months since my father had passed away and my break-up with Samantha. I had been feeling really down. Jean and Rita were amazing, and we got on really well. I especially liked Jean. He was just a few years older than me with a mad shock of Einstein hair and a warm, welcoming smile. In fact, we got on brilliantly. Rita was also an amazing woman; she was very motivated, flamboyant and confident and believed we had a great story to tell. She even offered to fly me to Paris.

A few weeks later I decided to take Rita up on her offer and was put up in a luxurious apartment close to the (pre-fire) Notre-Dame Cathedral. Rita was busy the first couple of days working on one of her projects but provided me with a guide. Catherine was a beautiful young Parisienne with big brown eyes and brown shoulder-length hair that was blown across her face by the March wind. Catherine had an itinerary planned for my trip. We first went to the Louvre to see the *Mona Lisa*. It has been described as 'the best known, the most visited, the most written about, the most sung about, the most parodied work of art in the world'. Which is a problem. The line of tourists who had come to see the most famous painting in the world was at least four hours long. Patience is not really part of my make-up, so we never did get to see it, but we did get to travel to the top of the Eiffel Tower. I read up on it and became something of an encyclopaedia on Paris and its architecture. I loved how well preserved the city was. At the top of the tower there were people proposing to their loved ones and drinking champagne in celebration. I thought 'when in Rome do what the Romans do' and got down on one knee and proposed to Catherine. She giggled like a schoolgirl and said yes. By the time we'd reached ground level our fantasy marriage was over and she was back to being my guide. It was all good fun.

Rita met up with me the next day and took me on a shopping expedition. As I got to know her, I discovered that shopping was by far her favourite pastime. I enjoyed the break, ate good food and even sampled frog's legs. I also began to feel a little bit better about myself, realising the trip had done me the world of good. My relationship problems were, for the time being, left back in the UK and not at the forefront of my mind. I went home feeling refreshed and grateful about the project these people were committed to. I felt safe that my story was in the hands of people who believed in me.

Roy and Sol had worked on a few small projects but this was going to be their biggest to date. They had at least managed to generate a lot of interest from overseas, spending lots of time promoting and trying to get financiers on board to raise capital at the many film festivals they attended. We had a director, a producer, a leading actor – all we needed now was the money to make it.

So when Charlie decided to leave the project we were all knocked sideways for a while. Jean, however, soon got busy and started the search for a new leading man, sending me pictures of various actors, some of whom I recognised, others I'd never heard of. One of the favourites with producers was Shia LaBeouf. He looked the part but was American and it didn't feel right to me.

Joe Cole is a young British actor who was in a popular TV series called *Peaky Blinders*. Jean emailed me a showreel. He asked me what I thought of this young guy playing Billy Moore. I liked him immediately. He had a look that was menacing but also could be sensitive and vulnerable. I had watched a movie a few years ago called *Offender* and remembered that the young guy I was looking at was the lead role. I saw myself, uncomfortably, in my youth. It wasn't a great movie, but Joe gave a powerful performance. Apart from *Peaky Blinders* he wasn't that well known, and so the producers weren't keen on him, worried they would not be able to raise enough capital on his name alone. Jean wasn't interested in big hitters and asked me to help get Joe Cole on board. He wanted authenticity, not Hollywood CGI rubbish.

'This is our Billy Moore, oui?' said Jean, who was keen to have him as a star, but he needed me to persuade Roy and Sol. 'Together we can do this, oui?' he said in his strong French accent.

I agreed that Joe seemed right; there was something about him I liked and he was up for a challenge and interested in the role. Jean wanted me to speak with him personally, which was arranged for the following Sunday via a phone call. Joe was great to talk to and I could feel his sincerity and humble attitude. It was all down to the producers now. After a while, Roy and Sol reluctantly agreed. Now we had our ideal lead actor, the project was back on track. Jean and I were pleased with the outcome; the next step was to arrange a meeting with Joe.

I was excited when Roy and Sol told me they had booked Joe into a hotel in Liverpool and that we would all have a meal. We arranged to meet at Joe's hotel and my first impression was how young he looked. It was awkward initially for both of us, but as the evening went on, we got chatting like a couple of old friends. We spoke about *A Prayer Before Dawn* and he told me he wanted to do it justice. When he asked how I felt about him taking on a Liverpudlian accent, Roy, Sol and I all looked at each other in bemusement. It was a hard thing to attempt, we all thought, but he was adamant he could pull it off. He wanted to add to the authenticity of my story by portraying me as accurately as possible. Roy thought it was impossible and mentioned that every actor he'd seen trying to mimic the scouse twang ended up sounding like John Lennon. I admired Joe for his passion and didn't mind at all. He wanted to spend more time with me to study me and develop a character. We arranged to meet on the set of *Peaky Blinders* in the next couple of months.

This was becoming all too exciting for me and I found, as time went on, my ego becoming inflated. My social media platforms started to become more active and I received a vast amount of friend requests and followers, plenty of who were beautiful women. Some even proposed to me. It was all surreal and I found myself burning the candle at both ends, answering them on Facebook. I still craved attention and felt the need to be desired, anything to change the way I felt, but really all I was doing was putting a plaster over a disaster. Women seemed to be the answer to all my problems and it stopped me from thinking about myself, but only for a short while. Romance and finance are the top offenders for an addict of my kind. I was soon going to find that out.

Chapter 8

Drifting

*We that are true lovers run into strange capers; but as all is mortal
in nature, so is all nature in love mortal in folly.*

As You Like It Act 2, Scene 4,
William Shakespeare

THE film project was taking shape so I should have begun to find
some meaning and purpose in my life. I had a job, a book and
a movie deal and should have felt happy and contented. Instead I
found myself drifting in and out of multiple relationships, never
feeling settled or happy with anyone in particular. I still felt betrayed
and deeply hurt by my ex-girlfriend Samantha and the way she had
treated me. I didn't want to be with any one person for fear of being
hurt, so I started to play the field. I'd begun to lose respect for myself
and, sadly, was losing respect and trust for others. That didn't stop
me looking for love though. Maybe I'd find my true soulmate, I
thought, if I managed to wheedle my way into enough women's
beds. Again, how wrong could I be.

I stopped talking to my friends at the meetings, didn't go for
coffee or meals with them any more and became a little obsessed

with my fledgling fame. A big mistake for someone with an addictive
personality like mine. I'd skip meetings or, when I did turn up, I was
late or would sneak out early feeling judgemental, intolerant, angry
and resentful. Spending money, going shopping, seeking out women
for sex – none of these would satisfy the feelings of emptiness.

I didn't know what was wrong or what was missing in my life but
I was trying to look for something. Whatever it was it eluded me,
and the pain continued every day. In some ways I was in active
addiction; using without actually using. Drug addicts explain how
this is known as a spiritual relapse – being sick and tired of being sick
and tired. I was descending into a dark, dark place. Of course, I had
no idea it was going to get a lot darker.

Flattery and attention from an attractive young woman, stroking
my ego and telling me how I deserved happiness, caught me unawares
and at my lowest ebb. She was the wife of a guy I knew and in better
circumstances I may even have become friendly with him. But I was
about to ruin any such possibility. Theirs was not a happy marriage,
or so I was told. She was in recovery like me and even attended some
of the same meetings. Smiling family photos on Facebook were a
charade. The occasional friendly text message became daily
encouragement. A casual meeting in a coffee shop led to more. One
early evening, she came round to my house for a casual drink and
soon was sitting next to me on the sofa signifying things might go
further. *Whoa!* I thought, *this can't happen*, and showed her the door
– both of us feeling sheepish and not a little embarrassed. She asked
if we could still be friends . . . A couple of days passed with more
exchanges of text messages. And the inevitable happened, but it
would remain our secret. As she was heading out the door to a
waiting taxi, guilt swept through me and I told her that this could
never happen again. One was too many – a thousand never enough.
The text buzzed my mobile the next day.

'Billy I need to get honest with my husband and tell him what happened between us. X'

What the fuck's going on here? I thought. *How could she do this to me? How could I do it to myself?* I tried to call her back, but it went straight to voicemail. What had I done? The next morning there was a message from the girl's husband.

'You shagged my wife,' it simply said.

The feelings I was experiencing at that moment were overwhelming guilt, shame, fear and also anger at how I had been manipulated by his wife. I had to respond but what could I say? Blame was usually my escape route out of situations I had got myself into. I felt disgusted at my behaviour. The damage and harm I had done to someone else through my intolerable actions plagued me; the consequences would ripple through the addiction fellowship in the coming weeks.

I discovered that I wasn't the first or the last person to sleep with her, but in a way I was the fall guy. Her marriage was on the rocks and the blame needed to be placed on someone. It took a while for me to build up the courage to apologise to her husband and also for him to be willing to accept my apology. We met up and, after I had done my best to humbly make amends, he thanked me and then surprised me by giving me a hug. It was emotional for the both of us and of course I was relieved, but that didn't make me feel any better.

I had learned an important lesson and realised the damage I caused. Still to this day I shudder at the thought of how I acted out. I'd done things selfishly just to change the way I felt, not caring about the consequences, and all because I didn't feel good about who I was. Sometimes having money, a home, a job and plenty of followers who regularly stroked my ego wasn't enough. I still thought the grass was greener on the other side when I should have been cultivating the grass under my own feet. Maybe the next chapter of my life was my own karma, the what-goes-around-comes-around kind of karma coming to bite me on my backside and shake me to my core.

Chapter 9

Cancer

This sickness doth infect
The very life-blood of our enterprise.

Henry IV, Part 1 Act 4 Scene 1,
William Shakespeare

SUNDAY evening and I was getting myself ready to go out and meet Francesca, a pretty girl of Indonesian origin. This time I had made sure she was single, but that didn't really matter. I was still looking for someone to fix me – even love me. I looked in the mirror and noticed a huge lump on the right side of my neck that seemed ominous; it had suddenly appeared from nowhere. I was quite shocked at the size of it and was confused about what it was. It looked hideous and my whole neck looked out of shape. How could I impress Francesca looking like this? I called her and told her I would have to postpone our date, explaining reluctantly about the lump in my neck.

Concerned, she offered to go to the walk-in medical centre with me. We waited our turn for the nurse in among the usual mish-mash of nosebleeds, coughs and colds as well as injured brawlers. She wasn't sure what the swelling was and called one of her colleagues. Between them they still had no idea and decided to call an emergency doctor. By this time, I was getting really worried. The doctor examined me and also struggled to diagnose the problem and suggested I see my own GP. This was ludicrous. It was obviously something. Francesca was wonderful and stayed with me the whole time I was there. We left, had coffee in the late-night McDonald's then said goodnight. Some first date!

A couple of days later I was sitting with my GP in her office, being examined and answering questions. She too had no idea and said she would make an appointment at Broadgreen Hospital to have a specialist look at it within the week. I was getting worried by now, especially since plans were in place for me to fly out to Thailand to join the crew who had started the principal filming of the movie. It seemed like an age before the day arrived for me to visit Broadgreen Hospital.

Sue, the skin specialist, poked and prodded at my neck. 'Is there any pain?'

'Nah, not really. I only realised it was there when I looked in the mirror,' I told her.

I was scanned and sat waiting for the results to come back. Forty minutes later I was back in the consulting room. Sue had been joined by a colleague and they were both looking at the X-rays in every possible position.

'What does it look like to you, David?' Sue asked.

'I think it's a blood clot in the neck muscle due to a tear,' he stated.

I felt relief sweep over me. It wasn't anything serious, I thought, and to be certain of his diagnosis David called in a senior colleague for his opinion. He agreed with the assessment.

'So, what's next?' I asked.

'The clot should work its way out in at least six weeks. It seems likely you've injured it in the gym. I'll give you an appointment to come back for a check-up in three months.'

'I'll just be getting back from Thailand then,' I said, smiling as I walked out of the room.

Manchester airport check-in and I was clutching my ticket. Travelling light, I had just a cabin bag stuffed with essentials. I'd pick up cheap clothes in a Thai market. I was confident enough in the Thai language to haggle with market-stall traders.

As the check-in girl scanned my passport through her electronic device, I caught a flicker of concern cross her face. Her professional welcome smile had dropped a little. As she pleasantly asked if this was my first trip to Thailand, her hand slid under the counter. I had begun to stumble over my answer when a more senior-looking colleague materialised and started to scrutinise my passport. Had I perhaps been 'in a little trouble in Thailand before?' he asked. Maybe I had 'overstayed my visa on a previous visit?'

I started to blag my way through, but as my anxiety levels went through the roof, the security officer unsmilingly handed me back my passport and realised I wasn't going to Thailand.

Although I was dejected that the Thai authorities had blacklisted my passport, thus denying me entry, I also gave a sigh of relief. What if my history of my last time in Thailand had been picked up *after* I'd cleared the first stage of immigration in Bangkok? What if I'd been on Thai soil when their security services and police clocked my return and decided to kick up a fuss? Memories of my last three years in Thailand, the rotten and unbelievably violent jails, overwhelmed me. Notwithstanding my disappointment at not being able to join the film crew, I shuddered at the thought and fled home in a taxi.

★ ★ ★

There was a letter on the mat. The hospital was insistent that I call them to arrange a further appointment without delay. The number I had to call was for the oncology department. This was not good. I was there at nine the next morning having a needle stuck into my neck for a biopsy.

Another very long week went by before I got a call from the hospital on my mobile; I made an appointment for the next morning. Although I was prompt the consultant wasn't – he'd been called away to another location so could I 'possibly come back in the afternoon?' My nerves were already shot from the past week's waiting and I couldn't bear the thought of even a few more hours in this state of uncertainty.

'Would it be possible to speak to him? I've been feeling quite anxious for the past week and it would really help if you could help me out a little. I won't be able to make it back this afternoon as I'm quite busy today,' I asked the nurse manning the reception.

'Hang on, I'll see what I can do.' She picked up the phone and dialled his contact number.

I thanked her and waited while she talked to a disembodied voice at the other end of the phone. She looked up at me and then back to the phone, 'The doctor really needs to speak to you in person. Would it not be possible for you to return around three?' she asked me.

'Why? What's wrong? What does he need to see me for?' I was feeling slightly panicked.

'I'm not sure but he really does need you to come back,' she said.

'It's not possible. Can he just tell me over the phone? I need to be at a funeral in the next half an hour, so I would appreciate it,' I said with more urgency in my voice.

She spoke into the phone again then asked me to follow her to a separate room so the doctor could speak to me in private. I followed her with a sick feeling in the pit of my stomach. The nurse handed me the phone. I took it from her and remained standing.

'Hello, is that Mr Moore?' a male voice asked me.

'Yes, speaking,' I said, waiting for the next sentence with bated breath.

'This is Doctor Smith. I am the consultant dealing with your case.' He paused then continued: 'I really wanted to see you in person but I hear you have other prior engagements.'

'Yes, that's true. I have a funeral to attend. I'm sorry I couldn't wait until the afternoon to see you. Is there a problem with the results?' I asked nervously.

'Unfortunately, it's not good news. The biopsy we took last week detected abnormal cells.'

Shocked and in disbelief I sat down.

'Mr Moore, are you OK? Are you still there?' the tinny voice said through the phone that was now in my lap.

I knew full well that 'abnormal cells' was a euphemism for Cancer – with a capital C.

'Yes, I'm still here. So what steps do we take next?' I asked, regaining my composure and trying to accept that I had cancer.

'We need you in theatre this Wednesday. We need to take a full biopsy to find out what type of cells we are dealing with.'

The nurse set about booking my appointment for 9 a.m., giving me instructions about not eating anything for twenty-four hours beforehand. I did my best to pay attention but the information passed right over me. I left clutching an appointment card and headed out to pay respects to the passing of John, the father of a good friend, uncomfortable in my grey fitted suit.

It was a little after 10.30 a.m. and I was in the car park when my phone rang. The screen said 'MY MUM' in capitals and she was calling to see how I got on at the hospital. Shit! I was going to have to break the news to her. I was afraid to answer, so I just let it ring out. I didn't want to worry her if I could help it. I was relieved when she didn't call back straight away, as it gave me time to breathe and process things.

I walked briskly through the car park and located my little Polo. I got in, leaned back in my seat and stared unseeing out of the windscreen. I took a few deep breaths and tried to fathom what the doctor had explained to me: it was cancer. *Shit out of luck*, I thought. Yet, call it divine intervention, something had stopped me from flying out to Thailand for three months the week before.

The phone rang again, shaking me from my reverie. I knew it was going to be my mother without looking at the screen.

'Hey, you OK?' I said.

'Yeah, I'm fine. How did it go son?' She sounded tired.

I paused before replying.

'Er, yeah, I'm fine, nothing to worry about,' I lied, not sounding at all convincing. My mother went quiet for a moment.

'Well, what did they say? Tell me, son. I know when there's some-thing wrong.'

'He told me I have cancer!' I said it as calmly as possible. 'But it's OK. Don't be worrying,' I said as an afterthought.

'OH MY GOD!' she screamed, 'Oh Billy, where are you? I need to be with you.' Now she was sobbing.

'Mum, it's OK. I'll be OK. Just calm down. Please.'

My heart was breaking hearing her so distressed.

'Oh please, Billy, where are you, son? I'll meet you now, I need to see you,' she pleaded.

'OK, stop this now. This is not going to help either of us and once I've finished what I'm doing I'll come and see you,' I said.

'Promise me?'

I was gentler in my response and promised her that I would see her later.

'I love you, son.'

The line went dead and I stared at the screen as the tears welled up, mouthing the words, 'I love you too.'

I sat alone in the car and gathered my thoughts. I wanted to be in the moment because I knew that, in the moment, I was OK.

The surgeon had to perform open surgery on my neck while I was wide awake. I had no anaesthetic owing to my poor veins: years of injecting drugs into my body had taken its damaging toll. I felt ashamed watching them repeatedly try and fail. The numbness in my neck was all that protected me from the physical pain. The minutes felt like hours. The doctor was leaning over me, yanking and pulling on my neck. All I could do was grit my teeth and hang on. The female nurse looked at me with compassion; I could see how her eyes smiled behind her surgical mask. I was suffering. It was probably the most frightening experience you could imagine, the tears were burning my eyes and the tension in my jaw caused stiffness.

Finally, the surgeon had completed the biopsy. My smiling nurse commented about how brave and quiet I had been; little did she know I was screaming inside the whole time.

The drugs I was given for the pain afterwards felt good – free drugs on the NHS, prescribed by a doctor and very much needed. Being an addict in recovery and self-medicating wasn't a good idea.

Chapter 10

Philippines

As roused with rage with rage doth sympathise,
And with an accent tuned in selfsame key
Retorts to chiding fortune.

> *Troilus and Cressida* Act 1, Scene 3,
> William Shakespeare

THE island of Cebu in the Philippines and we were shooting the final scenes of the movie. I was to spend nine days there and we had three days to shoot so I hoped to get some sightseeing done before being on set. The hotel wasn't the best, but it was probably the best our budget could afford. At least the bedroom floor didn't crunch with the sound of popping cockroaches when I stepped on it and the toilet was more than a hole in the ground.

Cebu prison was world-famous for its dancing inmates. They had millions of hits on YouTube for their Michael Jackson 'Thriller' performance which had become a worldwide phenomenon. My own experience in prison involved fighting, not dancing. Before ending up in Chiang Mai Central Prison in Thailand I had earned my living as a boxer, and once inside I'd had to use my fists to defend myself, and others, on many occasions. Westerners were often targeted by the Thai gang members. After one particularly vicious fight, I found myself enrolled into the prison boxing team. The prison resident boxing trainer – the *ajarn* – known as Chamnan or Nan, had coached and trained me for a showdown exhibition match to take place in the centre of the prison on the occasion of Songkran – the Thai New Year. My opponent was a hard fucker and feared by the rest of the boxers on Nan's team. His name was Pon, by far the best Muay Thai fighter and boxer in Thai prisons. The fight – in front of a baying audience of inmates and guards – had been bloody and tough. Pon and I had fought each other almost to a standstill – until I knocked him out in the final round.

On the day of the fight the weather was muggy and the temperature high, into the thirties. Pon was already waiting when I stepped into the ring. Nan massaged my arms and shoulders in readiness. The announcer introduced us both to the crowd. The crowd cheered to give us a warm welcome. We touched gloves before the bell sounded.

I came out jabbing fast, but Pon was quick and parried my punches easily, countering with some of his own. I knew from years of experience that footwork was essential and I used mine well, moving in quickly, bobbing and weaving from side to side, feigning a jab and coming over the top with a solid, right cross, which connected with Pon's nose. Blood gushed from a cut on the bridge of his nose and spattered the already blood-stained canvas. Pon took the punch well, slipped to my left side and sent a crushing left hook to my kidney. The wind was knocked out of me and I dropped to one knee as the pain engulfed me.

The ref began counting me out – one, two, three, four . . . I was back up by the count of eight. I wiped my sweat-drenched and bloody gloves on my vest and held my hands up high to show the ref I was capable of defending myself. To my relief the bell sounded, ending the first round.

In the corner, Nan looked concerned: 'Billy, you OK?'

I breathed heavily. 'Yeah, but my old injury's playing up, I guess,' I told him. I looked over at Pon, who stared and smiled at me in triumph as if the fight was over and he had already won.

'No look. Pon ladyboy,' said Nan.

The bell sounded for the second round. I kept my guard up and my elbows tucked in tight to defend my body. Pon attacked me hard and fast again, connecting with solid punches on the side of my head. He was dancing round like a young Muhammad Ali, and every time I tried to counter with my own punches he was gone in another direction. If I was to have a chance, I needed to cut him off, corner him.

Once I had him, I unleashed a solid combination of uppercuts and hooks, but his guard held strong. He caught me again on my left side. This time I grabbed hold of him, afraid to let go, not wanting to go down again.

'Kwai!' Pon spat through his gumshield. I was breathing hard, my lungs gasping for air.

The ref got between us and broke up the clinch. 'Chok,' ('Box') he shouted. It was difficult to box with Pon. He was a southpaw and led with his right, so I moved to my right, making it hard for him to pound me with his powerful left cross. Pon moved in quickly and fired off a right uppercut that jolted my head upwards, then smashed me in the body. The bell finished the round but Pon continued with his onslaught of body punches. The crowd booed.

I sat on my stool as ice-cold water was poured over my head and body. I was tired. Nan was speaking but I couldn't hear what he was saying. My left side hurt. Something didn't feel right. Nan slapped me around the face and said, 'Billy, last round OK!' When I stood up the crowd were screaming my name.

'Nan, why are they screaming for me?' I asked, confused.

'Pon, he no good man. People no like cheat.'

The bell sounded for the final round. I came out, guard down in a showboating style, head poked forwards, pulling faces to taunt Pon. He charged forwards angrily, wide open. He threw a jab. I rolled under it and caught him under the chin with a beautiful left hook – knocking his gumshield out of his mouth – and then followed quickly with a solid right cross. Pon hit the canvas. The ref stopped the fight and sent me to a neutral corner and counted . . . eight, nine, ten.

Pon was out. The crowd cheered.

Cebu prison was an ideal venue to recreate the epic fight. We were going to build a boxing ring in the middle of the prison yard. Marco, the prison governor, was himself a local celebrity. Years before, he had been an inmate in the very prison of which he was now the boss. Charismatic and larger than life, Marco's trademark automatic pistol lived in a black leather holster on his side while his T-shirt promoted gun use! Nevertheless, he made us feel very welcome, giving us access to the whole of the prison for our filming. As well as the boxing-match scenes, Jean had arranged for me to play a cameo role as my own father visiting his son while in Chiang Mai prison.

Joe Cole, playing me, was uncanny in his portrayal. He remained in character the whole time we were filming. The skinny lad was now muscular with cropped hair, seldom smiling and with an almost arrogant attitude. He practically ignored me as he became immersed in the part, speaking in my own northern accent. *Meet Billy Moore*, I thought.

Away from the prison, I found the Philippines remarkably similar to Thailand. While the film crew were setting up, I played the tourist, visiting a few islands, immersing myself in the hustle and bustle and admiring the pretty girls. At least here I felt more confident they were girls and not ladyboys. The discernible difference I noted was the prevalence of signs of Catholicism and not the Buddhism of Thailand.

In the evenings, back at the hotel, Jean and I met up with some of the cast and production crew. Somrak Kamsing was the only Thai to win a boxing gold medal in the Olympic Games; he was playing Nan, my boxing *ajarn* and mentor in prison. Somrak spoke no English so we got by in Thai and, like Nan, he smoked far too much and loved to gamble. Fight coordinator David Ismalone had taught Vin Diesel how to be a Muay Thai combatant during *The Fast and the Furious* movies. He had turned Joe Cole from a skinny white kid into the muscular fighter I had been in my prime. It was great to meet everyone who had been a part of the project from day one. As we enjoyed meals and chats my worries and troubles, even my cancer diagnosis, seemed to evaporate in their company. One evening, after Jean had enjoyed a few drinks, he wanted to hear what happened in a part of my story that I had never fully explained. When I had been busted by the police and arrested in Thailand, I'd hidden – in the time-honoured drug-concealment fashion – a whole stash of pills and cannabis up my arse.

This is a question people tend to ask me after reading my first book. OK, so let me take the opportunity to explain and add a bit of clarity to what really happened. I remember it like it was yesterday. After the police arrested me, I was placed in the back of the police car, handcuffed, confused and desperate. I needed drugs to function and I had none, except the tablets and cannabis I had up my arse, but they weren't my drugs of choice. I needed opiates, sleepers, downers; those were the kind of drugs that helped me to function. I had some money and asked the police officers to take me to the chemist. I told them I needed medication due to my recent motorcycle injuries, and lifted up my top and pointed to the left side of my abdomen. The police officer next to me visibly grimaced and spoke in rapid Thai to his partner. 'Where you need go? You need yaa na?' I nodded and pointed towards the city, directing them as we went. We parked outside a special chemist I knew who supplied methadone, Xanax and diazepam. I had about 2,000 baht on me and ordered three 50-ml bottles of concentrated methadone, forty Xanax, twenty-five blue and twenty-five yellow diazepam. They were handed to the police officer in a big brown paper bag like they were groceries.

The heat outside was immense; by now it was around early afternoon as we headed to the police station. Inside the lock-up I was taken to a huge dimly lit cell that held a couple of young Thai men. The only other light came from a small bulb in the corridor. The cell door banged shut and a voice from behind me said, 'Farang, you take.' I looked back to see the officer who had arrested me and taken me to the chemist holding the brown bag out towards me. He was handing me all the drugs. I simply couldn't believe my luck. I grabbed the bag from him before he changed his mind, ran to the other side of the cell thanking him as I went. I found a place to sit down, looked in the bag and, to my surprise, all the drugs I had purchased were still there. Oh yes. I took out a bottle of methadone and drank the full 50 ml, then popped a few blues, a few Xanax, and while I was at it a couple of yellows too. The two Thai guys came over, curious as to what I was up to.

'Pi me yaa, na?' the older of the two asked.

I showed them what was in the bag but they didn't seem interested. The younger guy imitated smoking ya ba – a mixture of methamphetamine and caffeine – and then gave me a toothless grin. 'Pi you have, na?' the older guy persisted, I nodded and smiled, 'Me kraph, ow mi?' They both nodded vigorously.

For some unknown reason I was wearing a leather waistcoat with tassels on it, and on the back was the picture of a huge American Eagle. It was something you would find on a Hells Angel riding a

Harley Davidson. The older Thai guy was admiring it. I stood up and moved over to the toilet to retrieve the tablets I had hidden up my back passage. The two Thai guys had a lighter and some chewing gum foil; they were prepared and ready to smoke some drugs. I placed a couple of tablets down between us and left the rest of them by my side for later. Only there was no later, because the police were suddenly back to take my prints and a photograph for their records. I left the drugs with the two guys as I was escorted from the cell.

It was sometime between the police sorting out what they needed from me and returning me to the cell that the medication I had not long taken began to kick in. The effects were potent to say the least. I had taken enough to knock out a small elephant and from then on everything was a blur. I awoke some hours later, feeling groggy, and in my confused state I struggled to recall where I was. I blinked away the sleep and rubbed at my eyes to try and focus properly. The first thing I noticed was the two Thai guys sitting up wide awake, looking like two meerkats; the older guy was wearing my leather waistcoat. I suddenly remembered the events from the night before. The tablets? Shit. Where had they gone? The bastards had smoked them, it was written all over their scatty looks. The brown bag of other drugs was still there, so I quickly grabbed it, looked inside and let out a sigh of relief. At least *they* hadn't been touched.

'Where the fuck are the pills?' I screamed at the two guys. 'And what the fuck are you doing with my jacket on?' I said, outraged at the cheek of it all.

Both of the guys looked shocked and a little scared. The older Thai pushed one solitary tablet, a lighter and a piece of foil my way. It was obvious what had happened, and, in truth, if the shoe had been on the other foot, I would have definitely smoked their drugs. My mouth was dry and I mimed drinking water. One of the guys quickly passed me a half-empty bottle of water. I gulped it down and realised all was not lost: I still had the ounce of Thai stick weed secreted for later . . . I kept that quiet.

Back at the Philippines prison the following evening, with the filming of the boxing match and my father's visit to the prison scheduled for the following day, Marco invited me to watch a dance. This I had to see. The YouTube videos had me in awe so I could only imagine what the real thing would be like. The dance troupe got ready as I stood next to Rita preparing to watch, and the excitement I was feeling was hard to contain. First, they performed a Michael Jackson number: it was so powerful. Everyone was in complete unison as they danced, and it was absolutely outstanding.

When they finished, Marco asked if I'd like to join them and have a dance. Wow. I couldn't believe my luck. I dashed as fast as I could down to where they stood, and Rita joined me. The music began to pump out loudly from the speakers positioned around the prison yard. I stood in line with a few of the guys who were all wearing orange jumpsuits and followed their direction. I was a lousy dancer compared to their professional moves, but I didn't care. This was a dream come true. Everyone cheered us at the end and it was nice to see Rita enjoying herself too. She was a beautiful woman and I felt glad for her happiness.

I was asked to speak to the prisoners and, out of breath, I took hold of the microphone. I thanked them from the bottom of my heart for a truly amazing experience – a once-in-a-lifetime opportunity. I spoke about families, prison and drugs, and shared my experience about what was important. There was a life beyond their wildest dreams and it was called freedom and hope. When I mentioned that crime didn't pay and that their families were more important, over three thousand inmates cheered and roared. It was one of the best nights of my life. Giving something back to so many was a gift.

The next day the ring had been built in the centre of the prison; it was hot and the sun beat down relentlessly on our heads. The stark reality of the Thai prison was here.

The time came to have my role portrayed in the movie. The scene was set and my nerves were shattered. I paced up and down in the prison waiting room, thinking about what I would say to my younger self if I was my father. Jean was there to coach me and assured me everything was going to be fine. It was now 5 a.m. and the final moments of filming were about to take place. I leaned against the window separating the visitors and stared intently ahead waiting for Joe – 'my son' – to arrive. The director tapped me on the shoulder then shouted 'Action!'

The memories of my father came rushing back just as Joe entered the visiting area. My emotions were high and I felt the tears gently brimming in my eyes. The room had a dim light that cast a shadow across the entire cell – it looked so authentic, but felt surreal. All I wanted to hear from my father back then was 'I love you, son.' Nothing else mattered and nothing else was needed. The unspoken words spoke volumes, the silent look and the honest regret I felt at that moment were real. For that moment, I was my father and I knew that I truly loved my son.

It was strange that I was playing the role of my own father, who had died of lung cancer, and now here I was standing before myself with my own diagnosis. It was a poignant moment in my history that was captured forever, and it was also a celebration of his life.

The filming of *A Prayer Before Dawn* was a truly beautiful experience but also emotionally draining. It was good to see the film finally come to fruition. As Jean, Rita, the cast and crew said their farewells, I too said my goodbyes, only just holding back the tears until I'd got through passport control at Cebu airport. After all the editing and final production was done, my next involvement was to be, fingers crossed, on the red carpet at the Cannes Film Festival.

Chapter 11
Relapse

0 my lord, Press not a falling man too far! 'tis virtue:
His faults lie open to the laws; let them,
Not you, correct him. My heart weeps to see him
So little of his great self.

Henry VIII Act 3, Scene 2,
William Shakespeare

RELATIONSHIP break-ups, poor coping skills and an intolerance towards spiritual principles led me down the path of a relapse. On top of this came my cancer diagnosis; that was the straw that broke the camel's back, the perfect excuse to use drugs. This was my fall from grace, on top of crisis after crisis, suspected meningitis, mental health issues and a whole shitload of problems. None of this justified using or my behaviour. The many illnesses and infections I contracted owing to a poor immune system led me to seek guidance from a healthcare professional. He prescribed barbiturates – a strong sedative – to help me relax and they were combined with opiate-based pain-killers. I wasn't sure I needed them, but I wasn't going to refuse, and if they were prescribed by a medical practitioner then surely it was OK.

I was five years clean, no smoking, using or boozing before I picked up drugs again. With years of experience in recovery, a part of me knew I should have known better. The bottle stated clearly what the correct dosage and frequency were. However, one tablet every two hours became three, then four and then six, until the whole packet was gone. I justified and minimalised my prescribed use, telling myself the doctor did say take them when needed, not when I wanted. I took more than what was needed, way more, even calling my sponsor and manipulating him to agree it was OK and not a problem. Somehow, that made me feel better. I only shared the bare basics; my inner demons had me on the ropes and lying through my back teeth. I called the doctor for repeat prescriptions. He would understand – how could he refuse me? I had cancer! He never did refuse, so I found it easy to continue my pill-popping activities. The consequences were not yet apparent in my day-to-day behaviour, so nobody seemed to question me.

I convinced myself that everyone was sympathetic to my cause, even encouraging me to keep taking the meds. I would never actually tell people I was abusing my medication in case they rejected me. I became addicted fast, popping more pills. Cigarettes soon became another habit of mine – everything went hand-in-hand when I picked up drugs. I no longer cared.

I realised that the pills had stopped working. I needed more than the doctor would prescribe. I began to buy more medication on the black market illegally, even from local drug addicts: boxes of diazepam costing £20 each. I thought more and more about picking up heroin. I was already on a roll with the prescribed and unprescribed meds, so fuck it, I thought. This would be taking my using to another level, maybe it would be different, maybe I could handle it this time.

I kept everything about my drug use a secret. It was a war I kept to myself and I was losing the battle: picking up drugs became my only option. I remember many years before someone asked me that if drugs were my answer then what was the question? All the clichés I'd heard over the years pricked at my conscience: your using will never be the same, you'll have a belly full of drugs and a head full of understanding. Still that didn't stop me wreaking havoc all around me.

The darkness of my soul was a portrait of my misery. Who could I call? It had been years since I'd used street drugs.

I blamed many things, everything except myself, for being reintroduced to opiates. I told myself 'just one' but that was a lie; the first one always did the damage. Again another cliché popped into my head, that one was too many and a thousand was never enough. The overwhelming loneliness I was feeling, along with the emotional pain, was crucifying me. An old familiar voice whispered in my ear, 'We can make this go away, Billy.' It spoke to me in my own voice and I recognised the liar returning, making promises that would never be kept, robbing my soul and harming everyone in my path . . . 'NOOOOO!' I screamed, covering my ears tightly with both hands. It was on me, the obsession was too great, my defence system had fallen apart.

I was going to use drugs, and nothing and no one was going to stop me. I reached for my phone and called Ebby. He answered on the third ring.

'All right, Bill, what's happening?'

'I need you to score for me,' I said, and then added, 'It's not for me, it's for our Judder.' I used my cousin's name and lied to avoid my own shame.

'I'll get you one of each, mate,' he said, knowing I was probably desperate for drugs. I was in the grip and nothing was going to stop me. He turned up with both the heroin and crack cocaine, feigned some concern and then left. He, like myself, was in the grip of addiction and powerless to say no, so I didn't expect him to refuse, but I knew he wouldn't feel good about it. The reality was we all found means and ways to get more of what we needed, friends or not.

The progression of my addiction was rapid. I was spending up to £100 a day to almost end my life. Drugs always led to consequences. I used on my own, ashamed and embarrassed of anyone finding out. If any of my friends or family became suspicious and questions were asked, then I would justify being on medication as the answer. I was already plotting, scheming and beginning to tell myself the most outrageous lies. I told myself that my drug use was a way of coping with my illness, that was the best excuse I could muster. I knew that there were two people in the fellowship who had cancer and stayed clean, but both had died and that's what scared me. At least they were brave and had the courage to face their fears and die clean.

I, who had fought my way through the streets, boxing rings and prison, couldn't find the courage either to face my own demons or face up to the possibility of dying. I had been diagnosed with non-Hodgkin's lymphoma – a form of blood cancer – and the hospital consultants had put me on a course of intensive chemotherapy. Over the months I found out the worst part of having cancer wasn't what it did to you, it's what it did to the people you love. I didn't want to speak to anyone. Using drugs for me always became the answer to the problems in my life. It was a great way to avoid responsibility – in a narcotic trance everything seemed manageable.

During chemotherapy, I would shake with fear as I felt the cold liquid seeping into my veins. Even for a professional phlebotomist finding a vein would be impossible and they would have to insert a PICC line – a catheter. I would take the journeys to the hospital alone, driving my car erratically, even falling asleep at the wheel sometimes. I was so tired and fatigued that I would sleep all day and became a chemo zombie. I spent a couple of weeks in hospital and I was the worst patient you could imagine. I used drugs in the hospital toilet, not caring about anyone but myself; in fact, not even caring about my own wellbeing. I would use alone on the stairs in the early hours of the morning, paranoid I would get caught by the night-time security. My drug taking was very uncomfortable and not at all enjoyable. I was eventually discharged back to my home, where I used even more. Hiding out in my bedroom, killing myself slowly, giving up on life. *What was the point anyway? Why me?* I thought. Then immediately I thought, *Why not me?* I would travel to the hospital as an outpatient for chemotherapy and spend a total of seven hours with a drip hanging out of my arm. I spent most of the time there on my own; no family, no friends, just how I liked it, drugged up and unconscious.

Days, weeks and months passed by in a drug-fuelled blur. The phone would constantly ring, people would constantly knock, family and friends were concerned about me, but I just didn't care. The well of depression consumed me; I was sinking fast. I couldn't eat and I isolated myself an awful lot. My cousin Gary knocked one day, shouting my name through the letterbox, and refused to leave until I answered.

I eventually opened the door and was greeted with a warm smile and a huge hug.

'Ya ma's worried about ya, lad. Get in touch with her and let her know you're OK,' he said, voicing his concerns.

'My head's wrecked with it all, mate,' I said, resigning myself to my own demise with a self-pitying view on life. The blame-thrower was out with a fuel tank full of depression.

'You need to get your shit together, mate. Have you tried the cannabis oil? I wish my ma'd had the chance to use it. She'd still be here today, lad,' he said with a heart heavy with loss and sadness.

'No, why? What use would it be for me?' I asked, curious as to its benefits.

He pulled out his phone and began to show me all kinds of stuff regarding cannabis oil and its healing abilities. Could this be my chance of survival? He spoke of conspiracy theories and got really deep about the whole aspect of it all. He gave me the number of one of his contacts who came to see me the following day with prices. He also showed me how to use it properly – using suppositories, cannabis and coconut oil. I paid £400 for one month's supply. This was the price one had to pay for another shot at life. Cheap for those who could afford it. I was also given some advice about my diet, told to avoid sugar and maintain acidic foods.

Roy and Sol had organised a benefit night to support me in funding the cannabis oil I needed. I felt that they had messed me around on my contract and gave me a poor deal in the process, so I guess they felt guilty. The night would involve a banquet, a raffle and a talk with me and Joe Cole. I looked terrible. All my hair had fallen out and my weight had plummeted. Tickets had sold out and a lot of support came from friends and members of the recovery meetings I attended. Actors from *Peaky Blinders* came, including Joe's younger brother Finn and Paul 'Boycey' Anderson. Stephen Graham, an actor from Liverpool who grew up with my cousin Gary and who went to the same school, popped over to my home the day before and donated some signed photos and memorabilia. The support I was receiving was overwhelming. It was quite surprising who had turned up: Colin Martin, the author of *Welcome to Hell* on his time in the Bangkok Hilton, came to offer his support, winning and buying almost everything. I liked him and we got on well. He was as mad as a box of frogs. Jay, my old friend from Essex, travelled up to see me and stayed in my home. It was an emotional evening with friends, family and colleagues showing solidarity. The money that was raised helped towards the expensive cannabis oils I needed; my heart oozed with gratitude.

However, the money from the benefit night couldn't last forever. I found out YouTube was a great way to learn new ideas and cultivating cannabis was one of them. I could make my own weed to smoke and use the leaves to make the oil I needed. I didn't want anyone but Gary to know that I was planning on growing cannabis in my home. I needed some guidance and with a renewed excitement I contacted him and asked for advice. He gladly offered to assist me as he was a heavy pot smoker himself. He would benefit in not only helping a member of his family to try and recover from cancer, he could also smoke the profits. We discovered how to access the mysterious dark web, which was the perfect way to buy all the stuff we needed in complete secret. We bought a hydroponic tent, lights, fans, the nutrient Canna Coco A & B, the whole works. All we needed now were the seeds. Gary suggested Alien OG auto-flowering seeds as they would only take nine weeks to grow. I ordered them online and received them in less than three days; we had everything set up, the pots and soil were ready and we germinated the seeds ourselves. All we had to do now was set the timer, shine a light on them and wait for them to bloom. I enjoyed the tasks and it kept me occupied, distracted from the thoughts of dying. The clouds shifted a little. I was fighting back.

Daily, I continued to take the oil I had purchased; at least I was giving myself a fighting chance at life. My using continued against my will but I would soon get around to quitting once I was ready, I kidded myself. For now, I continued to cultivate cannabis, justifying it was only for medicinal use and not for sale. No one knew of my small enterprise apart from Gary. I became a little obsessed and bought two more tents with all the equipment. I now had two in the spare bedroom and one in the loft. The OGs seemed to be growing well. I became a little bit of a cannabis connoisseur as time went on.

Chapter 12

Olivia

For what is wedlock forced but a hell,
An age of discord and continual strife,
Whereas the contrary bringeth bliss,

Henry VI, Part 1 Act 5, Scene 5,
William Shakespeare

CANCER is a shit show. It's a disease that rocks you to the core.
People sent me messages that confused me. They told me to keep fighting. I knew they meant well but how can you fight an enemy that you can't see? This is more than just an invisible war; this is going in blind. The only way I knew how to fight was with my fists, so that's what I did. I put on a pair of gloves and I hit back. The cancer became my punchbag. This allowed me to stay focused and in control. We all fight our battles in different ways. People call me courageous, brave and a fighter but I'm not: I'm an addict and I'm scared. So, I used and abused myself with copious amounts of drugs to avoid thinking about dying.

What I didn't comprehend is that I was killing myself in a different way, mentally and spiritually; all that was left was that piece of me within that never ever gave up. Alone I drowned out the thoughts with a cocktail of drugs and slipped into an unconscious world of unfeeling, a dark place where thoughts and fears didn't exist. I liked it there, but I didn't belong there.

The months passed and I had finished my last round of chemotherapy; now came the six-to-eight-week wait for the results. Too long. I was still working but couldn't tell my employers as I was sure they would terminate my contract. I needed to access some clinical support as the fear they would try to sack me had me constantly worrying. My head was all over the place and I couldn't think straight. I had met a girl – someone I'd known for a while but never expected to date.

Olivia was blonde with high cheekbones and the looks of a catwalk model. She enjoyed the gym and taking care of herself. She worked for the Civil Service, lived alone, had no children and was thirty. I was surprised when she got in contact with me via Facebook Messenger one evening to ask how I was. One, I was shocked she did and, two, flattered when she told me she'd fancied me for quite some time. *If only she could see the state of me now, I'm sure she would change her mind*, I thought. After talking and getting to know more of each other, we arranged to meet at her home for coffee one evening.

I felt insecure about my image so drank a half bottle of brandy before I turned up, and swilled my mouth out with mouthwash and sprayed myself in tons of aftershave to mask the smell of the alcohol. All my weight had gone, all the hard work I'd put in at the gym to build up my muscles was gone, and in its place was nothing but skin and bone. The cancer treatment meant I was completely bald by this time and felt ugly. I was still the same person she'd met almost a year ago, she told me; my illness didn't change who I was inside. Olivia saw past the illness and focused on the interior landscape, making me feel a little more at ease within myself. We began dating – a big mistake.

Alarm bells were ringing from early doors, but I dismissed the warning signs of yet another impending disaster. Love is blind as well as silent and with my track record for meeting women who were totally unavailable it would probably end terribly, another toxic broken heart.

But maybe this new relationship would give me the motivation to get clean. I really liked Olivia, mostly for how she looked – I was always a sucker for a pretty face. I couldn't understand what she could see in a man with stage-three cancer who had relapsed into addiction. I was vulnerable and in need of a bit of love but for now I was just going to roll with it.

I had no idea what the outcome of the blood tests would be. The denial of it all and the drugs kept me oblivious to the seriousness of my problems. Olivia's presence in my life kept me occupied. She was sometimes difficult to be with and I routinely blamed myself for our petty arguments, always feeling the need to apologise for being in such a poor state. I knew I wasn't perfect, but I increasingly became aware of her odd behaviour.

Her text messages and demands to support her were relentless. I was in no position to support myself, let alone Olivia, and was being made to feel guilty just for being me. Some days when I was alone in my own house, I'd find myself wandering from room to room screaming aloud for help or motionless on my bed sobbing. The truth was I was a complete mess – and this had to be the lowest point of my life.

I phoned an addiction service, hoping they would help. They offered me an appointment for that Wednesday. Then they suggested a detox on the Friday and that gave me hope. I needed to stop using opiates for at least twenty-four hours so the doctor could provide me with Subutex, a different opiate to help with withdrawal. I finished what drugs I had left that day and prepared to sit it out until Friday, only to be called twelve hours later to be told I would now have to wait until the following Monday. My hopes were dashed; the only window of opportunity I had was now gone. Monday? I needed help now, today, not fucking *Monday*! This was shit. I was using deadly amounts of heroin and crack cocaine. I now weighed nine stone and looked like a bald, wrinkled bollock. A small boy completely lost in his own sadness. The phone ringing shook me away from my thoughts. It was Olivia.

'Hey, you OK babe?' Olivia said, rooting for me all the way.

'I'm not really but what can I do?' was my dejected reply as I related my latest wretched tale.

'Billy, do you *want* to live?'

'Of course I do,' I said, before sobbing uncontrollably. I was beaten and broken.

'Well, get a cab over to me and I'll help you with your detox. Just do it. Get in a cab. Don't worry, I'll pay for it.'

Relief swept over me. I wanted to surrender and thought it was a good idea to detox at Olivia's. She had experience in nursing and had just promised to support me. I'm not sure what she was expecting but it was going to be a rough ride for the both of us. I arrived at her place about an hour later, absolutely shattered, and fell straight into bed. I didn't wake up for over thirty-six hours. It was a living nightmare, but Olivia was true to her word. I was doing it raw so you couldn't even call it a detox, it was a hardcore withdrawal – a rattle – without medical assistance, which was very uncomfortable. For the first three days I stayed in bed, hardly moving, while Olivia was busy working in her home office during the day and all I could stomach was fluids; any solid food I tried to eat came straight back up. By now I knew my appointment with the oncologist was on 8 February when I would be given my final test results. Unsurprisingly I was worried and deeply pessimistic after the war I had just put myself through.

My movie had recently been selected for the Cannes Film Festival

– the most prestigious film festival in the world – but still I couldn't get fucking *clean*.

'Billy, at the end of your life story when the credits begin to roll, do you want them to read that sadly, before the film had been distributed, Billy died in active addiction? Or that Billy fought cancer and he is now living a healthy life, helping others become motivated in their recovery?' Olivia had a beautiful way with words.

The day of my appointment with the oncologist arrived and Olivia was, as ever, supportive in accompanying me to the hospital. I sat in the room waiting for the news, preparing myself for the worst and truly believed this was *it*: flat broke, in debt, nothing left to fight for. I had resigned myself to my demise.

'How are you feeling, Mr Moore?' the oncologist asked me.

'Prepared,' was all I said in response, unable to look up.

'Well, the results are back and I'm glad to say you have cleared the cancer.' He had got straight to the point.

It didn't register immediately. Had I heard him correctly? *I'd cleared the cancer?*

'What do you mean, I'm going to live?' I said somewhat shocked, having readied myself to break the bad news to my family.

I looked at Olivia and found myself crying unrestrainedly; she gave me a hug and said nothing, allowing me to come to terms with things in my own time and recalibrate my feelings. Not only was I clean and abstinent from all drugs but was also in remission from cancer. No longer did I have to hide my shameful addiction. This was my chance to move on with my life one day at a time.

Or so I thought.

Chapter 13
Rob

If I must die
I will encounter darkness as a bride,
And hug it in mine arms.

> *Measure for Measure* Act 3, Scene 1,
> William Shakespeare

B IG George was from Glasgow and a good friend. He was in recovery and had been clean for twelve years at least. We had met at a convention in Warrington a couple of years earlier and had become friends immediately. He was one of the funniest guys I had ever met: a big man with a bald head and round glasses who spoke in a strong Glaswegian accent. His stories about the Zombie Bee Gees, the double-denim junkies, would have everyone laughing to the point of incapacity. That was *his* recovery: watching other people's spirit come alive through humour. After recently being given the all clear, I felt it was about time I started to reconnect with old friends. George wanted to spend a weekend in Liverpool with me and he asked if could he bring a newcomer called Rob. I thought that, after all I had been through, it would be nice to have the house full of laughter and good company. Sadly, nothing ever seemed to be plain sailing.

After only six months of recovery from his addiction to opiates, it turned out Rob had relapsed on his visit with George. We found him at the bottom of the road, slumped against a bollard. We tried to get him to go to the hospital, but he became aggressive, screaming and shouting at us both as if we were his enemies rather than his friends.

'I'M BRAND NEW, PAL! I don't want to go to no feckin' hospital,' he growled as we struggled to help him to his feet. He was a big guy, very intimidating and not someone you wanted to mess with. In the Glasgow underground he was known as 'Bulletproof Rob'. To make ends meet he worked as a doorman in the Glasgow pub and club scene, generally keeping order and sorting out trouble-makers, so you get the picture.

Slumped against the concrete bollard he didn't look brand new. His breathing was shallow, but he kept repeating that he didn't want us to take him to the hospital. He was adamant and it was his choice. Instead we did our best to keep him moving and took him to a meeting. He was physically mobile but out of it; he went to the toilet and people in the meeting were concerned and volunteered to keep an eye on him. Lee, a mate of mine, came over to me looking worried and whispering that Rob didn't look too good and that he was unconscious in the toilet. Lee helped George and me pick him up – walking him around the hallway. We suggested the hospital again and each time we did all it did was antagonise him and he refused point blank to go.

The meeting finished and as George and I drove back to my house it was all we could do to keep him awake. He was hungry and wanted a kebab but we were almost home, so I ended up cooking him some Scottish square sausage and tattie scones George had brought with him from Glasgow. Eventually we took him upstairs and put him in bed in the spare room, laying him in the recovery position. Outside the bedroom door we both listened to his loud garrulous snores and felt assured he was OK. He would sleep it off.

In the morning Rob was dead. He was well past help as rigor mortis had set in, his face blackened from lack of oxygen. Rob, thirty-eight years old, was father to two young children and had a large part of his life ahead of him. Now he was dead in my spare room. The police arrived and his age and sudden demise meant they automatically treated it as a suspicious death. We were both interviewed for more than nine hours in the front room of my house while Rob lay lifeless upstairs. The police eventually left, satisfied that it was an overdose, while George and I remained in shocked disbelief.

Well, shit! This wasn't on the cards. I was struggling with my own obsessions, having only just done a home detox. I was fifty-six days clean and just two days later I fell back into addiction and became embroiled in a brief but intense period of using that engulfed my whole being.

I would drive up and down the hot spots of Liverpool looking for drugs; this became my daily routine. Lying to my family, friends and work colleagues became as easy as breathing. The date for Cannes was less than two weeks away and here I was back in the grip of a continuous and progressive illness. I managed to disguise my drug use well, manipulating everyone around me. No one knew the secret shame I was hiding.

Chapter 14

Using

Abandon all remorse.
On horror's head horrors accumulate,
Do deeds to make heaven weep, all earth amazed,
For nothing canst thou to damnation add
Greater than that.

> *Othello* Act 3, Scene 3,
> William Shakespeare

I SPENT three hard months back in the grip of addiction. This time it was different: my family had cut me off, my mother had blocked my number and my friends refused to answer the phone. When they did, you could hear the dread in their voices. I would constantly lie to Olivia, telling her I was clean. She was adamant and told me to get at least ninety days drug free before she would speak to me again. I couldn't even get a morning clean so how the fuck I was going to get to ninety days? It was impossible.

One day Olivia surprised me by knocking on my door and shouting through the letterbox. 'Billy, open the door. I know you're in there.' She rapped even harder on the door as if I hadn't heard her the first time.

Shit! I panicked. I'd just scored some crack cocaine and was ready to have my first pipe of the day. Confused as to why she was at my front door, I hid the drugs and paraphernalia and ran downstairs in my nightgown, putting on my sick face . . . not altogether difficult given how drug use had made me look lately. I opened the door.

'Hiya! You OK?' I mumbled, then coughed to emphasise my (fake) ongoing illness, hoping she'd fall for my Oscar-winning death scene.

'Well, are you going to keep me standing here?' she demanded, obviously not impressed with my performance.

To be honest I didn't want to let her in; all I wanted to do was get back upstairs and use drugs, but also I didn't want to lose her or raise any suspicions. I was juggling secrets and manipulating everyone around me.

'No, no. Of course not. Come in. I just don't feel too good, must have caught a bug, you know with my immune system being low,' I said, coughing and hoping she'd believe my shit excuses.

Olivia stood in the doorway looking me up and down, shaking her head with pity and sadness reflected in her cornflower-blue eyes. I must have looked a sorry state indeed, standing there with my hair matted, pasty pale skin and a week-old growth. My forehead was covered with a sheen of sweat and I must have stunk to high heaven, because my body hadn't seen a bar of soap for at least a week.

'OK, get changed. You can stay with me tonight. We'll see how you are in the morning. If you're no better we'll get you a doctor and, don't worry, you can get a bath at mine,' she said, rolling her eyes. There was no escaping her. My preoccupation with continuing to smoke the small amount of crack I had left was killing me, but with all the insanity of an addict's thinking, I told myself I'd find a way.

'OK, OK, wait here. I'll be as quick as I can,' I said as I ran upstairs to my room with the intention of having a final blast on my pipe before we left for her house. A big mistake. As I was putting a flame to the crack on the cigarette ash, I heard footsteps marching rapidly up the stairway. *Fuck, fuck, fuck,* I thought. Panicking, as my eyes darted to the door. I rushed over, balancing my crack on the pipe like a professional circus entertainer, not dropping one crumb as I did. I couldn't afford to lose my next high. The door banged as I leaned against it.

'What's going on in there?' demanded Olivia.

'Nothing! I'm just getting changed,' I lied, stalling for the time it took me to light my pipe and thus ignite the ending of our relationship.

'Oh my God! Have you got a woman in there?' she screamed as she forced the door open with her shoulder, barging her way in.

A woman? A fucking woman was the last thing I was going to have hidden in my room.

The door crashed open and I was compromised in the act. The shame of being caught crushed me; this was powerlessness at its finest, loving someone with all your heart and soul and yet still not being able to stop. I stood there in silence. There was no defending what she'd caught me doing. It was over!

The only thing I was grateful for was the acceptance I felt about being caught. No more having to hide, no more lies.

She screamed, shouted and eventually cried while all I could do was hang my head in shame and hope she would leave so I could finish the rest of my drugs. The buzzing from the next room caught her attention. She stormed off and entered the bedroom where there was a cannabis farm. I stayed rooted to the spot as footsteps ran back downstairs, then a couple of moments later rushed back up. I still didn't move; it was only when I heard a crashing sound that I headed to the next room.

Oliva had cut down all the lights and had crushed all the plants, and now she was cutting up the tent with a pair of huge scissors she'd found in the kitchen.

'What the fuck are you doing?' I screamed, grabbing the scissors from her hand. 'This doesn't belong to me. You're going to cause murder,' I said, slumping against the wall in total resignation. It was true, it wasn't mine. I had moved on from my little arrangement with Gary and the tent didn't belong to me; it belonged to a local drug dealer I knew who wanted to set up a grow tent with a few plants and then share the profits with me. It was just going to be a nightmare to explain and had potential financial consequences. Something I was going to find difficult to handle.

'I should call the police then, because you're vulnerable and you're being taken advantage of.'

I was fuming and crying, slumped down against the door. She had no understanding (why should she?) of how her unthinking action would lead to potentially severe repercussions.

'Just go. It's over and we both know it,' I said, wiping away the crocodile tears.

Olivia stood over me, not saying a word, for what seemed like an eternity. Then, 'Get ninety days clean, Billy. If you love me, you'll do it.' She left me still slumped against the wall full of self-pity, slamming the door behind her.

My loneliness took me to some dark places, and I found myself spending the last of what money I had in crack houses. My companions became the dregs of society: shoplifters, beggars and prostitutes. These were the only places I felt accepted and sometimes, if not most of the time, I felt better than everyone else. How strange it is that your insecurities can have you feeling inferior to everyone on one day but, on the very next day, superior to those who are just that little less fortunate than yourself.

I frequented one crack den quite regularly that was inhabited by every social misfit under the sun who used drugs in and around my community. Here were some of the most damaged people, often very dangerous too. The front room was thick with a dense cloud of smoke and in the midst of it sat a bedraggled bunch of lost souls. The continual shouts, screams and arguments over drugs always resulted in someone getting badly beaten up. I sat on the top of the stairs while Ronnie and his girl Karen wrapped small amounts of heroin and crack cocaine ready to serve to the screaming horde who waited, behind a gated door, at the bottom of the stairs. Karen was in her mid-forties, but decades of drug abuse had aged her dramatically; she could have easily passed for an OAP, while Ronnie, who was a few years younger, with sallow skin and high cheekbones protruding from the tissue-paper-thin skin of his face, looked even older. Ronnie was one of the main drug dealers' front men and could shift a lot of merchandise daily. Massive amounts of drugs were sold from the top of those stairs and the only reason I was allowed to sit and smoke with them was because I looked intimidating and that made Ronnie feel safe as he went about his work. I wasn't complaining as long as he was throwing me the odd gratis smoke now and then.

Karen, who wasn't the brightest of sparks, opened the gated door one morning to get some water from the kitchen and left it ajar. Big mistake!

'Give me the drugs,' screamed a gangly guy who had run up the stairs and was now holding a knife to Ronnie's face. 'Give me the fucking drugs or I'll stab you,' he roared, foam frothing from his mouth. His skin was yellow, his teeth black, as were his bulging eyes. He looked frightening and in withdrawal. He hadn't noticed me as I stood in the doorway out of sight at the top of the stairs. As I stepped through the doorway I threw an uppercut, landing it right under his jaw and knocking him backwards. He fell down the stairs, tumbling to the bottom, where he lay in a heap.

Ronnie still looked scared to death and with a half-lit cigarette dangling from his lips asked, 'What the fuck just happened?'

'What happened . . . was he brought a knife to a fist fight,' I said as I sat back down, leaning my back against the wall.

'Why wasn't the gate closed, man?' he said, looking down at the still half-opened gated door.

'Ask your bird. Drugged up and getting sloppy on your supply, mate,' I told him.

'She's doing my head in. It's those fucking pregabalin tablets she's buying off everyone. They're sending her scatty,' he spat angrily.

Karen stepped over the prone body and came back up the stairs, holding a glass of water unsteadily in her hands.

'Here you go, babes, nice glass of water for you,' she said, unaware of what had just transpired.

'Shut the fucking gate, ya silly cow. We've nearly been robbed because of you,' Ronnie shouted, getting out of breath with his chronic obstructive pulmonary disease.

Karen screwed up her already thoroughly wrinkled face, which made her looked like a sucked prune, and screamed a string of largely incoherent obscenities back.

I'd gone past caring about myself. All I wanted was to get high and stay high, and if it meant I had to be a dogsbody for a two-bit drug dealer who was feeding me a constant supply, then so be it. I was lucky I had a home to go to at the end of the day, away from all the chaos and mayhem that I'd chosen to be a part of. The only reason I went there was for the company – it wasn't the greatest and most positive company, but I struggled being alone.

It was getting more and more difficult to be around the violence. It got worse as the weeks went on. Gunshots were fired through the window one night. The noise was shattering. It was lucky no one was injured or killed. Enough was enough. *Fuck this*, I thought. I jumped in my car and left to the sound of sirens screaming towards the house, vowing never to return, praying to a god that I didn't believe in to help me get clean. This nihilistic way of living – in truth, merely existing – wasn't for me any more.

How had it come to this? One minute I'm on the red carpet in Cannes celebrating my achievements; the next, I'm sitting in the most insalubrious places on the planet using drugs. This wasn't how it was meant to turn out. This wasn't how I wanted to be known. It had got me so low that ending my life seemed like the only option, but that was not the type of person I was; there was something still inside of me urging me to fight, and that was the reason I was still alive. Why, I didn't really know.

The loneliness I felt more and more was indescribably sad. Although I've had many rock bottoms in my life, I truly believed this to be my worst. This wasn't one of those rock bottoms where I could carry on that little bit longer, or die that little bit more. The lies would usually open up more trapdoors and bury me even deeper in the abyss of my self-made hell. This time, I somehow knew this was it for me, this was the true rock bottom. The progression of my active addiction had almost fucked me – physically, financially and mentally. And it had tortured my family and ruined all my relationships.

I was grateful that, although I was running desperately low on money, I still had a car and a roof over my head, but while I had my problems with my addictions, so my landlord had to deal with his own issues. Drink was his nemesis and even though I had never missed a rent payment in three years, his drunken rants and demands for payment had become routine. There was only one occasion when the rent was overdue – when I was in hospital! The landlord took to harassing my friend to pay it. On the day I got out of hospital – feeling weak and vulnerable – he was banging on the door and threatening me, 'Pay up or else!' Despite me telling him in no uncertain terms to fuck off, I was perfectly aware it needed to be paid, so I went out to borrow what I could and pawn most of my remaining possessions at the nearby Cash Converters.

On the way back an hour later, as I turned into my street, I was confronted by several police cars lit up like Christmas trees and gun-carrying armed response police in flak jackets and stormtrooper helmets. *What is going on here?* I wondered. This is exciting! Really fucking exciting as I found myself face down on the pavement and my arms behind my back as the handcuffs were snapped on my wrists. It was outrageous!

My landlord had phoned the police claiming I'd threatened him with a huge knife. Not true and not fair. Fortunately, despite my history with the police, my protests of innocence were believed, as there was no evidence to suggest I had a knife. Not so for the landlord – after another three made-up complaints over the next few weeks, he found himself arrested and facing charges of wasting police time.

Most of my possessions had been sold for drugs. Every penny I had was gone and all my credit and debit cards were maxed out. I broke into the home of my neighbour (who had never done me any harm) and stole items to fund my habit. I was absolutely broke and internally destroyed. The last days of my using had become terrify-ingly desperate; I sat alone in my darkened bedroom, afraid of a knock on the door. Afraid of everything. I made a slow, conscious decision to reach out and ask for help. I had already emailed my employers and told them of my relapse but had received an instant response telling me they were on annual leave for two weeks. I needed help now. I was beginning to do things against all my morals and principles. I resented everyone and blamed society as a whole for my current predicament. My mind was distorted, and I believed in my own paranoia. I didn't want to wake up any more.

I couldn't go on any longer, hurting others to feed my selfish needs. There was a part of me that wouldn't give up, that knew there was a way out if only I had the courage to ask for it. I emailed Rita and poured my heart out to her, telling her everything, and from that moment on my life changed because I chose to take responsibility for my poor decisions and shameful actions.

Rita and the film team were sympathetic and understanding, and decided to help me. They paid for me to go to rehabilitation. It was a private clinic in Essex called The Gateway Recovery Centre that worked a twelve-step programme of recovery. I was grateful beyond words. My admission date was less than two days away. Bernie, my lodger of five months, helped me pack up a few of my personal possessions. He had been great company and I was sad to be leaving him behind. I wished him well and pleaded with him to get some help; he promised me he would. We filled the car up as much as we could before parting company. I gave him a big hug and told him to get his shit together, jumped in my car and drove to my mum's little bungalow to wait for my transport.

The rest of my possessions were dumped or sold by the landlord, I later learned. I have no forgiveness in my heart for this person; he had preyed on my vulnerability for more than three years. He was the most vulgar pisshead I had ever met.

It was time to take that step back into recovery and start taking care of myself and discover why I had flipped the self-destruct switch again. Olivia, my long-suffering partner, helped me although she hadn't spoken to me for over two months. She knew I was putting my decisions into action and she respected that. It took her, my mother and friends to distance themselves from me in order for me to hit rock bottom, allowing me to crawl out of my personal hell. No longer were they prepared to enable me to continue to use; at the time I resented them, but in hindsight they all helped to save my life.

I arrived at my mother's at 5 a.m., a total wreck. It had been months since she had seen me; she took my clothes and placed them in the wash and told me to get a shower. I had taken my last bit of heroin and popped twenty tramadol pills a couple of hours before I had arrived, and I was shattered. There was a quilt on the sofa ready for me and a steaming bowl of tomato soup.

'Why do you keep doing this to yourself, son?' Mum asked. 'You should know better. What's wrong with you? It's breaking my heart to see you like this. You were doing so well. I can't understand why you went back to the drugs,' she sighed.

'I don't know, Mum. I think I was just scared of everything. Believe me, I don't want to be doing what I'm doing. I'm not enjoying this way of life.'

'Well, you're going to get professional help now. You'll be OK. Just stick it out and come home safe,' she said. 'Now get yourself some rest. The taxi will be here at 9 a.m. I've left a few ciggies on the kitchen table. That's your lot, don't be asking me for any more. I'm going to bed to get a few hours. I'm bloody knackered. I love you and I'll see you when I get up.'

I lay there for a few minutes before sleep took me. My dreams were lucid and before I knew what was happening the morning light was shining brightly on my face.

Chapter 15

Rehab

In poison there is physic; and these news,
Having been well, that would have made me sick;
Being sick, have in some measure made me well.

Henry IV, Part 2 Act 1, Scene 1,
William Shakespeare

It was 12 September 2017 when I took the long journey from Liverpool to Essex, in a taxi. We left at 9.30 a.m. and arrived some six hours later. I was in a state of exhaustion, so they showed me to my room where I collapsed on a queen-size bed before immediately falling into a deep dreamless sleep. This was going to be my second stint in rehab. The previous time I was in a rehabilitation unit was thirteen years earlier and it was government funded, so this was going to be a totally different experience, a five-star experience. *This should be fun*, I thought. I was certainly not five-star material and had Olivia to thank for sourcing a rehab, paid for by the team of producers. I could still hear her telling me that this was our only chance at maintaining our relationship. 'This is it, Billy! Last-chance saloon,' she warned before I headed off to rehab.

The doctor prescribed me Subutex for heroin withdrawal. For the first three days I was in absolute agony, vomiting, shaking and unable to move, and my bedsheets were drenched in sweat. I screamed for help. I was hallucinating, angry with anyone who came near me. On the fourth day there was a knock and a middle-aged woman popped her head around the door asking me if I was decent. She introduced herself as Sandy, my therapist. She wore a bright red flowery cotton dress, hippie-style beads in her hair and metal-studded boots.

'Hi Billy, how are you feeling? I've heard you've been struggling with your medication. Is there anything we can do?' It sounded like faux concern to my cynical ears.

'Yes, I'd like to see the doctor. The meds are not enough,' I said, shivering on my sweat-sodden sheets. I was hunched in a foetal position, fully clothed with my tracksuit hood up.

'Yes, of course. We can arrange for you to see the doctor this evening. We are here to help,' she said smiling.

'Thanks,' I grunted.

'We need you to join us for morning meditation in the group room, Billy. Can you manage that?'

Is she fucking nuts? What the fuck is she going on about? Meditation? I need fucking medication, not fucking meditation.

'Are you serious? I feel fucking terrible,' I croaked.

'I'm sure you're finding it difficult, but you did sign a compact, Billy, when you came in . . . ' she said, becoming less accommodating and more assertive. 'Come on, you'll feel much better once you're out of bed.'

'For fuck's sake . . . ' I huffed, forcing myself out of bed. I wasn't in any mood for this shit. How on earth could anyone meditate during a detox? It was impossible. I followed Sandy towards the group room and upon entering noticed all eyes on me. It was the first time since I'd arrived that I realised there were others in the rehab unit – up until now I had been wrapped up in bed, isolated and well away from everyone else.

I sat, pulled my hood up and avoided eye contact. Quiet Andean pipe music began to emerge from a pair of small speakers: the meditation group had begun. I could see that a few of the clients had adopted the lotus position – going for meditation gold. I couldn't be arsed with all this; I wasn't mentally or physically ready and felt I was being pushed too quickly into a bunch of holistic therapies that I had no affinity for.

Once the meditation session finished, I went downstairs and forced myself to eat some breakfast. The rest of the group were outside smoking in the shed. I followed suit and bummed a smoke from a tall cockney bloke with glasses who introduced himself as Tom. He seemed nice enough, and others spoke to me and made me feel welcome. Someone asked me what I had been using and I told them I was on heroin, to which I heard a fat bloke in shorts and tank top shout in a London accent, 'So you're a smackhead then?'

Cheeky bastard! Who the fuck is he calling a smackhead? I let it go and took a huge drag of my cigarette. The next thing I knew I spewed projectile vomit, spraying the whole interior of the smoking shed with blue and creamy bile. My breakfast had made an unannounced appearance to the disgust of the guy who had just insulted me.

'Fackin' 'ell!' he yelped, as he rushed away holding his nose.

I fell to my knees and continued to throw up – eventually nothing but yellow bile. I kept muttering under my breath, 'I'm sorry, I'm sorry.' A hand grabbed my elbow and pulled me up. It was Tom.

'You're OK, bud. I know exactly how you feel. I'm nine days into my detox. Morphine sulphate. Same shit, different drugs, but the subbies have helped me loads,' he said with a wry smile.

'I need to lie down, mate. I don't feel so good,' I said, walking in the direction of my room. I couldn't even manage the short flight of stairs to the second floor so waited, hunkered down on the bottom step, for the disabled lift.

''Ello, Bill. Fack me, son, you look like you've been through the wars,' said Neil, the head therapist at the Gateway and someone I had known for a number of years. Neil was an Essex boy and in recovery. He had used drugs the same way I had. He was just staying clean a day at a time like I used to.

'Hello, mate,' I managed to croak, suddenly feeling both entirely embarrassed and deeply emotional.

'Come 'ere, mate, it's OK,' he said, giving me a huge welcoming hug. 'You're safe now.'

'Thanks . . . it means a lot,' was all I could say.

'Bill, it's not that often we get the real deal, maybe one a month, but fack me, mate, you're the real deal, my son. Now go and get yourself some rest. I'll send someone up to see you with some orange juice.' The lift door opened, and I got to my room and fell into bed. I was definitely the real deal compared to most of the clients in here. I was a hardcore heroin user and had no one wiping my arse with £50 notes every time I fucked up. This was basically the only chance I would have to get clean in a five-star treatment centre.

The doctor saw me that evening and upped my meds. I knew I had to do this detox, but I was finding it really difficult. Out in the garden that evening I apologised to the guys for spewing my guts. Fortunately, everyone seemed fine and laughed it off. I got chatting with a few of the residents: there was a pop star's dad (his son was in a world-famous band that even I had heard of . . .) who had arrived that day and was still fucked. This was his second stint there. Then there was George, a young, fat, tantastic gay guy from Essex who became quite fond of me and who had enduring problems with cocaine. In fact, most of the clients were there for cocaine and alcohol addictions. These people were paying £3500 a week for therapy; my planned rehabilitation was for six weeks including my detox, and this was the only chance I was ever going to have of getting my life back.

Sandy summoned me the next day for a one-to-one therapy session. She wanted to discuss my childhood, but I wasn't going down that road again. I knew why I had relapsed and I knew what I needed to do. First things first: I needed to get through this detox successfully.

'Billy, you need to attend meditation and a process group every morning. You'll be in group A. It's important you engage or you'll receive a warning . . .' she said, making me aware of the consequences.

'OK, no problem. I've just been feeling rough for the past few days,' I said, knowing this was my only chance.

We had to identify ourselves as addicts or alcoholics and speak from 'the I and not the We' in our process group. There were also a number of other groups such as dialectical behavioural therapy, or DBT for short. It was a form of cognitive behavioural therapy (CBT) and was basically mindfulness. Then there was my favourite: the twelve steps. I already had some knowledge and understanding of them.

In the rehab, Caroline was a pot smoker and while her using was a vicar's tea party compared to mine, she was one of those rehab junkies who knew the lingo and would use it in every fucking sentence.

'I'm powerless.'

'I'm unmanageable.'

'I would like to challenge you with regard to your behaviour.'

'I would like to make a vulnerable request about the washing machine.'

I would like to make a vulnerable request about your vulnerable request, I thought. She was like an AK-47 on a tripod and loved the sound of her own voice, to be the centre of attention, a proper drama queen – and not only did she piss me off but did the same to everyone else with her controlling attitude. Miss 'fucking-let's-all-meditate-for-two-days' was a cosmic job and an emotional womble! So, you probably guessed it – we didn't get on. I was so glad she wasn't in my group. I mentioned this to Neil who told me she fancied me. Fuck that! She looked like Olive from the 1970s sitcom *On the Buses* and, to be honest, I wasn't exactly in the loving mood; my sex drive was non-existent.

The rehab was in a small, picturesque English town and was surrounded by beautiful green fields. The smell of the countryside was in the air. Days were long and boring and in the evening we sat around either smoking and chatting in the shed or watching TV in the lounge. I would struggle to sleep each night but knew this was part and parcel of the consequences of my detox.

There were a few young guys there. One talked about getting drunk a lot and it seemed like a good idea to me. He gave me some money after I had approached him about getting some alcohol from the local off-licence in the town. I dressed all in black like Milk Tray Man and headed for the back gate, climbed over it, avoiding the cameras, and swiftly walked into town. *What the fuck am I doing?* I asked myself. *What if I get caught?* It was too late: I was already at the door to the off-licence and heard myself asking for gin and soda for the Brummie and brandy and coke for myself. I tucked them in a bag and headed back to the rehab as quickly as I could. Somehow, I managed to get back in without being seen. I hid the bottles at the back of the smoking shed and crept over to the seats away from the cameras. I had only just breathed a sigh of relief when one of the support workers called me over to the patio.

"Ello Bill, we need you to do us a breathalyser,' he said.

'Me? Why?' I said, acting all surprised.

'Someone has been drinking, we've been told,' he said, looking me up and down suspiciously.

'That's me fucked then,' I laughed.

'Why? Have you been drinking?'

'Give me the breathalyser and let's get this over with,' I said, feeling relieved that I hadn't had the chance to drink the alcohol yet.

That night I sat in my room and drank the brandy and the next night I drank the Brummie's gin. That was the last time I used. My first day clean was 23 September 2017 and I was well into the swing of things by then.

Sandy wasn't my cup of tea; she was too flower-child-like and ethereal for my tastes.

'Billy, isn't it wonderful to be clean and sober?' she would ask me in our therapy sessions.

'I'm clean, not sober, that's for members of AA,' I reminded her. 'How could anyone be clean and sober? Does that imply you could be clean and drunk? No,' I said defensively.

'You should embrace your sobriety,' she said with a huge earth-loving smile, paying no attention to my thinking.

'Whatever,' I muttered. The therapy I was receiving was useless; I was grateful, but it wasn't what I needed. All I wanted was somewhere safe to stay – just for a while.

That day our group was dialectical behaviour therapy. Sandy and another female therapist gave us an instruction manual and took turns in leading the group. Sandy, her long black hair in braids, was dressed like a child of the sixties, as was her wont, finished off with a pair of elaborately ornate cowboy boots.

'Hi guys. How y'all feeling today?' she beamed, adding to her odd, confused Wild West/bohemian vibe, her smile a masterclass in insincerity.

'Billy, how are you doin'?'

I sat shivering in the corner wishing she would get on her high horse and ride right out of town.

'Like shit,' I growled. How else was I supposed to feel? Happy, joyous and free? I was at the height of withdrawal, and the only feelings that were surfacing were anger and pain.

'Billy, you sound angry . . . let's talk about it,' Pauline, the other therapist, said. She too was in possession of a phony 'customer service' smile. Why the fuck was everyone pretending to be so happy?

'I'm not feeling too good and I can't be arsed with all this shit,' I said. It was still early days and I wasn't in the best shape, to be fair.

'OK. Non-aggressive stance, Billy. Can you see what I'm doing?' Pauline said, with her palms facing outwards and a radiating toothsome smile on her face.

'And what the fuck does that mean?' I asked, confused. Both Sandy and Pauline walked towards us with one foot out and palms facing forward.

'Right guys, this is a non-threatening stance we can all use to defuse volatile situations,' Sandy said.

'Billy, why don't you try it? The evidence tells us that it is proven to work successfully,' Pauline offered hopefully.

'Listen, that's complete bullshit. If I attempted a "Hi, my name is Billy and this is my non-threatening pose" shit in a crack den in Liverpool, I'd get stabbed in the eye before I could utter the words, "It's all cool, brother,"' I said, receiving laughter from some of the more streetwise members of group.

The session ended and I went back to my room. The therapists had meant well but in truth we lived in different worlds. The clients there had money with access to all sorts of safety nets while I had nothing apart from an ex-girlfriend's North Face hoodie and worn tracksuit bottoms. Most of the group members, let alone the therapists, hadn't used like I had, had never been exposed to the levels of degradation and desperation I had witnessed and lived through. I found myself judging them by my own lights, but what right did I have to judge? To be fair, we had all travelled down the dark road of addiction whether we had money or not.

Lawrence was a young black guy from north London who came into the rehab. He was the real deal; you could tell he was a full-blown junkie. We got talking about recovery, using and the nature of despair; the therapeutic value of one addict helping another was my pathway to freedom. Lawrence had been living on the streets and his mother was crying out to have her son back. She had used up all her savings to send him to rehab for four weeks and it was costing her almost £16,000. He knew this was his only hope of getting his shit together. I liked him and spent most of my time sharing my own personal journey, rediscovering my enthusiasm for life as the days went by.

I had smuggled my phone into the Gateway and hid it successfully in my room. Switching it on, I discovered a message from my mother asking me to call her as soon as possible.

'You OK, Mum? What's wrong?'

'Billy, Walla's just come back from your house. The landlord's changed the locks and the neighbours have just pulled him and told him you burgled their house. They have you on camera, son.' She sounded resigned. Disappointed rather than angry.

I didn't know what to say. I felt a sinking feeling in my stomach; this was all I needed. The memory I could retrieve of that fateful evening was annoyingly vague, coming to me in a succession of blurry, black-and-white photographs. My neighbour was on holiday – I knew this because his car had been gone for a few days. I'd awoken early hours one morning from a heavy night of drinking and taking drugs, still groggy and wearing only shorts and a T-shirt with nothing on my feet.

I find myself in the neighbour's back garden. I steal a few bottles of Prosecco from his shed where I also find, and put on, an old pair of sandals. I am attempting to climb through a window at the back of his house. Now there's the intrusive sound of an alarm going off. Panicking, I climb back over the fence into my own backyard and scurry indoors. I run upstairs to my bedroom and rapidly change into my pyjamas before going back downstairs to see 'what all the fuss is about'. The opposite neighbours are standing outside looking at the house, while the alarm blares. They stare through a mottled pane of glass in the front door and hold a bunch of keys while they talk in urgent whispers.

'What's going on?' I ask, pretending to rub sleep out of my eyes, exaggeratedly stretching.

'We think someone's broke into Kenny's,' says the concerned neighbour, a huge, overweight, middle-aged man with a shock of grey hair. 'He left us the keys while he was away,' he says nervously, having another pointless look through the window.

I remember agreeing to accompany the trusted neighbours as they checked the house. This was a perfect opportunity to steal anything I could conceal. It came to me in the moment . . . the stories of addicts stealing from people and being first in the queue to try to help the injured party find what had been taken. Welcome to my world.

It was the next day when I finally came to, after drinking the Prosecco and taking more drugs, and realised what I had done. It was wrong, it didn't feel right and it wasn't me. What had I become? I had broken into the home of a neighbour whom I'd known for more than three years and stolen his property. This is what happens when I take drugs: nothing matters and all I care about is where the next drug is coming from. I hated myself and beat myself up for the harm I had caused while in addiction. With a sounder, clearer mind, this would never have happened.

This was yet another problem on top of all the problems I was already dealing with: the guilt and the shame . . . was it never going to end? My life seemed one crazy mess. After the phone call from my mum, I lay on my bed thinking about the mistakes I had made while I was using drugs and knew I couldn't change the past. I said the 'Serenity Prayer' out loud: 'God grant me the serenity to accept the things I cannot change, the courage to change the things I can and the wisdom to know the difference.'

I knew I had to take responsibility sooner or later but right now I had to recover and focus on my treatment. I carried on the best I could but at the back of my mind the thought of being arrested and being sent to prison again niggled away. Olivia wouldn't be happy, so I decided to block it out of my mind and move forward. *What will be will be*, I thought.

I was coming to the end of the first stage of my primary treatment at the Gateway. It was difficult and by this time I was on my final warning. I was moved down the road to the main house, classed as independent living, with a cannabis addict named Elizabeth, gay George, Tom and the pop star's dad, who I never managed to get on with. His arrogance and self-centredness were too much for me to deal with. One day we fell out in a big way. I was doing my level best to conform to the rules. I had been clean for over twenty-eight days and was desperately trying not to get kicked out within the next (and final) eight days. In fact, I never made the graduation. Pop star's dad threatened me in a taxi one afternoon over a McDonald's hamburger. It was my control issues that got me into a volatile situation. Neil had told me not to divert from the afternoon meeting over in Colchester and had specifically insisted that I didn't go to McDonald's on the way back. I got a little paranoid when everyone asked the taxi driver to pull into the drive-through. I said how it wasn't a good idea, only to be met with resistance from pop star's dad. Things became heated and words were spoken.

'We're going to lock horns, me and you, when we get back,' said pop star's dad.

'I'll demolish you when we get back, you cheeky twat!' I shouted more aggressively than was necessary; he was pushing all the right buttons, this fella.

Sure enough, I was kicked out and soon on my way home in a taxi. I stayed clean regardless. I couldn't afford to use again, no matter what.

Chapter 16

Arrest

I'll haunt thee like a wicked conscience still,
That mouldeth goblins swift as frenzy's thoughts.

Troilus and Cressida Act 5, Scene 10,
William Shakespeare

THIS was it, my only chance. The producers were obviously disappointed when they learned I'd been ejected from the rehab and could only wish me well. I knew that if I didn't stop what I was doing – and stay stopped – then I would probably end up dead or in a closed ward for a long, long time. I stayed with a close friend, a cockney called Will who lived in Liverpool. He didn't take drugs and was willing to support me until I found somewhere to live.

I dreaded telling Olivia what had happened because I knew how she would react. I was right. She flipped and wouldn't speak to me until days later. While she was delighted to hear I hadn't relapsed, she made me make a solemn promise I'd never use again. I couldn't promise her anything: I knew that today I was clean and that was *all* I could offer. 'Yesterday was history, tomorrow is a mystery and today is a gift. That's why it's called the present.'

Each day was a battle. I only had thirty days clean of the drugs under my belt and found it a struggle to sleep, but I kept myself occupied and stayed connected to positive people. Soon I moved into an abstinence-based halfway house and attended self-help groups daily for something to do. I even began to get myself to the gym. I knew the police wanted to speak to me about the burglary and vaguely hoped they would simply forget all about me, yet in my heart doubted they would. I'd been arrested a week before going to rehab for drug driving and possession of a bladed article. While the drug-driving charge had been dismissed through lack of evidence, the outstanding charge of being in possession of a bladed article (namely a knife that I had in the boot of my car) remained. Mere possession was enough to have me charged.

I had recently been given a date for the Dublin Film Festival where they would be showing *Prayer* but I was due in court one week before the event. I arrived at court feeling confident the knife possession charge would be dismissed based on the location of the item. My solicitor soon dampened my optimism, explaining that wouldn't be the case as I was transporting the knife.

'But I was moving home – the boot of the car was full of my household goods.'

'Yes, I understand, but the magistrate presiding over your case won't accept it as a defence,' he explained. He then went on to emphasise that the current public outcry regarding knife crime might influence the magistrate to treat even this ludicrous charge with undue seriousness.

I found it hard to accept that the courts wouldn't acknowledge the facts: I wasn't 'carrying' a knife and in the forty-five years I'd been on this earth I had never been accused, arrested or charged with possession of a knife. I would always choose to use my fists before using a weapon.

'This is all because the police officer couldn't prove you were drug driving,' he told me.

'Well, they did try to take blood but after three attempts they failed to do so. It's not my fault that the chemotherapy ruined my veins.' I was already feeling resigned to pleading guilty and throwing myself on the mercy of the courts.

'What about the break-in? Any news of that yet?' Problem after problem seemed to be piling up and it wasn't doing my mental state any favours.

'No, but let's not worry about that today. First things first. Let's get this out the way today and we'll focus on that if and when you get arrested.' Maybe a little bit of hope on the horizon?

'How do you plead, Mr Moore?' the magistrate asked me. I noticed he had a very sharp nose.

'Guilty, sir,' I said reluctantly, knowing it was all a nonsense. I usually admit responsibility when I'm wrong but here I was pleading guilty to something I felt pressured into by my solicitor.

The magistrate listened carefully to the mitigating circumstances, even reading the supporting letters sent by my employers, Sandy my therapist and my cancer doctor. Magistrates are volunteers who hear cases in courts in their community and that's why those courts are known by criminals as a 'kangaroo court', a term some people claim means they 'jump' over evidence that might have helped the defendant. They can hear cases in the criminal court, the family court, or both. Each case is usually heard by three magistrates, including a magistrate who is trained to act as a chairperson plus a legal adviser in the court who gives direction on the law and makes sure the magistrates follow the right procedures. The three magistrates on the bench left the court to discuss my sentence. My solicitor was convinced it would be conditionally discharged owing to the sixteen-year gap since I was last before the courts and I was considered a man of good standing in the community.

'Please stand, Mr Moore,' said the chairman of the magistrates. 'We have thought long and hard about this case and as you know carrying a knife is a very serious offence. This court will sentence you as we see fit, following all the relevant guidelines.' There was a noticeable harshness in his tone of voice. I knew then and there I wasn't getting off with a conditional discharge and began to feel even more anxious as the proceedings continued.

'OK, sir,' I muttered, and lowered my head out of respect.

'You will receive nine weeks in custody . . .' he said, pausing to allow his statement to sink in ' . . . suspended for eighteen months. You will also be electronically tagged for four-and-a-half months and will pay costs of £220 to be paid to this court.'

Well, there was no mercy on offer that day; tagged in a halfway house and unable to attend the Dublin Film Festival. What more could go wrong, I wondered. Olivia was upset and wanted me to appeal so I did just to please her, not believing anything would come of it, but six weeks later, in the Crown Court, the conviction was overturned. It was too late as I had already lost the opportunity to go to Dublin.

It was a cold November evening and my tag had been removed the day before, giving me a little more freedom to get to more self-help groups. There was a knock on the door and, when I answered it, there stood two serious-looking police officers.

'William Moore?' the young female officer queried.

'Yes, that's me,' I answered, knowing exactly what was coming next.

'We are here to arrest you for a burglary,' she said and pulled out a set of handcuffs.

I shared the house with two young lesbian girls, Shannon and Claire, both recovering from cocaine problems and I got on well with both of them. They could see how deflated I was and asked the officer whether the handcuffs were really necessary. The policewoman and her male companion looked at each other and then said no, so long as I cooperated. *Thank God for small mercies*, I thought. I climbed into the back of the police van minus handcuffs and without being searched so I still had my phone in my pocket. The first thing I did was call Olivia. She wasn't going to be happy.

'Hiya, love. Are you OK?' I asked, trying to remain calm but feeling deeply worried. Burglary carries a minimum sentence of three years.

'Yes. What are you up to?' she asked, unawares.

'I don't want you to get upset but the police have arrested me for robbing the neighbour,' I said as if it was no big deal.

'Oh my God. You must deny it, Billy. They'll send you to prison and then what am I going to do? I will be a prisoner's wife!' she cried.

Deny it? I was bang to rights on CCTV. If I denied it and it went to trial, I would end up with five years at least. I had no choice but to admit it; the shame of what I had done had been killing me inside for nearly four months.

I was charged and bailed the same night and within a month I was back in the Crown Court for the plea, but it didn't go ahead for an odd reason. During the burglary I had stolen a small amount of jewellery that was now hidden close to my old house. My conscience was plaguing me, and I had decided to pick it up and hand it in to the court on the day of my plea. The judge looked shocked and hadn't a clue what to do. She would not accept the returned property on behalf of the court, so was forced to bail me for another two weeks with a tag. The judge explained this was the first time she had encountered anyone attempting to return stolen property to the court. She instructed me to hand it in to the nearest police station. Otherwise I would be rearrested for handling stolen property.

All I wanted was for this to go away. I was almost five months clean and these were the consequences I was facing for my behaviour when using. It was all my own doing and I couldn't blame anyone for the situations I found myself in. This is what happens to me – a drug addict – when I pick up drugs.

This was it. I was a prolific burglar in my youth with a record that was eight pages long. There followed a hard couple of weeks that had me thinking about every kind of escape from the situation. Once my solicitor told me I would in all likelihood receive a custodial sentence, I even thought about going on the run. All I could do was acquire a degree of internal acceptance and stay clean. I hoped my neighbours could find it in themselves to forgive me. The support I received from my family and friends was amazing. They all knew that in my right mind this would never have happened. Everyone got behind me and promised, no matter what the outcome, they would stand by me. That was enough to give me the strength to face what lay ahead. I still hoped the judge would find a degree of compassion and prove relatively lenient but, above all, I feared how I would cope being in prison for the first time without a dependency on drugs. I packed a bag full of clothes, bought a little HMP thumb-sized phone, and hoped for the best.

Chapter 17

Consequences

Nor airless dungeon, nor strong links of iron
Can be retentive to the strength of spirit.
But life, being weary of these worldly bars,
Never lacks power to dismiss itself.

Julius Caesar Act 1, Scene 3,
William Shakespeare

STANDING on a prison roof is a great way to get noticed. And that's what I wanted back in 2003 – to get noticed; to be acknowledged; for someone to look at me, see me for who I was, a small, frightened child who was never allowed to grow up. I was desperate and full of fear. I couldn't live life on life's terms; this was my only escape. I needed help. I just didn't know how to ask for it. To me, being on the roof was the answer.

Sadly, for the time being no one was about to ask me to tell them my life story; all they wanted was to get me and my fourteen fellow inmates off the roof. HMP Liverpool was on lockdown and seventy feet below us a full complement of guards in riot gear were spread out and craning their necks to look up at us.

Discontent had been bubbling all day. It was one of the hottest days of the year. The whispers went around: 'We're staying out, they can't make us go back into those sweatboxes.' There was a buzz of excitement, which mounted and spread from man to man like electricity. It was forbidden; it was a mutiny; we were going to defy the system.

At first they closed the gates, left us in the yard and watched us from behind barbed wire and seven-foot-high locked gates. They watched us the way people observe dangerous animals in the zoo. They said nothing.

There were about a hundred and fifty of us in the yard – the guards knew better than to try and take us on and aggravate an already explosive situation. They had all the time in the world. We took our shirts off and let the sun beat down on our pale prison skins. Big mistake! We wanted to get up on the roof – that was our objective and to get there we needed makeshift ropes.

Earlier, the word had spread quickly that something was going down in the exercise yard. Dinner time had come and gone without the usual queue of hungry inmates shuffling along, metal trays in hand.

'What's going on?' an inmate asked.

'What the hell's going on?' another shouted.

'A sit-in, in the yard,' came the reply from another group of inmates.

'Where?'

'In the yard, man.'

The screws were flapping around, yelling, trying to get the others back in their cells and away from the situation.

Back in their cells the guys wanted to be in on the action. If they couldn't get up on to the roof, at least they could help the men in the yard get there. Men started to pass sheets out of the cell windows.

Brown sheets floated down into the yard and were tied together into ropes. All we needed was a climber. Actually what we needed was Spider-Man, and we had him!

His name was Austie, a cat burglar with a stutter. He was a local lad who was game to try anything. He tied the sheets around his waist and got up on to the shoulders of the tallest man available. From there, he grabbed on to a drainpipe and, by getting his tiny feet into the smallest of crevices, he shimmied up the pipe. We watched breathless as Austie inched higher and higher. As we looked on, dirt and debris fell in our eyes and all around. He was getting there. Even the screws must have been impressed because, when Austie made it to the roof and stood with his hands in the air like Rocky Balboa, the whole prison erupted with shouts and whistles and yells of approval. That was Austie's finest hour, no doubt!

Three guys successfully made it up on to the roof, and then it was my turn. The last bit of climbing I remembered doing was when I was a ten-year-old and thieved eggs from birds' nests. I could hear one of the landing staff shout, 'No chance, fat arse!' and a chorus of sniggers from the other screws.

Fat arse? I'd show them. I scrambled up the sheets, helped by the men above who pulled me up as best they could.

At the top, hearing the jubilation, I felt like a superstar. But the thrill was short-lived. I was getting what I wanted, for sure. I was being noticed. But not in the way I wanted. Suddenly, I felt alone and scared. I knew I'd have to come down sooner or later and for a split second I contemplated taking the quickest route. For that moment I envisaged myself splattered all over the yard, my blood drying fast in the scorching heat, the detested screws having to scrub away the bits of me which would be plastered all over the walls and tarmac.

But that's not the kind of person I am.

147

In fact, I was brought down sixteen hours later in a cherry-picker, suffering from sunstroke. I spent a night in the hospital wing and then the next seven months in solitary confinement. I got a few kicks and a few punches from the guards – nothing I wasn't already used to. It was a bit of an anti-climax.

So much for my big cry for help.

Sixteen years later, life in HMP Liverpool – currently the UK's worst penal establishment – was very different. The news reports spoke of bloodstained walls, cockroach-infested cells and extreme violence. The news reports were right. This was the grim, notorious Walton Gaol, as it used to be known.

Here I was standing in the dock at Liverpool Crown Court, feeling anxious and hoping the judge presiding over my case would understand and be sympathetic towards events that led me to stand before him today, and praying that I wasn't about to be reintroduced to the joys of HMP Liverpool. I had written a letter to the judge explaining how my actions were totally out of character.

To whom it may concern,

Before sentencing I humbly request and would be grateful if your honour would kindly read a statement I have prepared for the court. Firstly, I would like to apologise to the victims of this crime. I am truly sorry for the pain and suffering I have caused them. I deeply regret my actions and the shame I have brought on my family and friends who have supported me through my illness, addiction and recovery. Throughout my life since childhood I have been a habitual criminal who was nothing but a drain on society until my late thirties, due to my drug addiction. In 2004 I had an opportunity to get clean in an addiction clinic in Somerset. I stopped taking drugs for a period of 3 years, then went to travel to Southeast Asia working as an English teacher and Muay Thai boxer to make ends meet. Having what I now know to be coping skills, I became embroiled in a relationship that I was ill-equipped to deal with to say the least. At that time, I didn't attend 12-step recovery meetings to maintain my personal development as was suggested whilst in treatment. This resulted once again in a relapse as past traumatic experiences were triggered once again. I ended up imprisoned in Thailand for handling a stolen mobile phone which was horrific. I received a sentence of 3 years for this in 2007 then I was repatriated back to the UK in 2010 to finish my sentence. On release I made a determined effort to get my life back together to which next is my testimony. I thought long and hard about what I could give back to the community and decided to volunteer initially to gain experience in an area which I believed would suit me best, so that others could benefit from my past experiences. I also began to write about my experience that didn't glorify addiction but was an authentic and honest account of my journey whilst imprisoned in Thailand. A book was published in 2014 and has since been made into a motion picture that is due for release in the UK in July 2018, which my family and I are quite proud of. As you may or may not be aware I was diagnosed with cancer, stage 3 non-Hodgkin's lymphoma in May 2016, this is in no way an excuse for my actions, however I was introduced back to drugs (prescribed opiates and benzodiazepines) from which I had remained abstinent since October 2011 by engaging in the 12-step programme of Narcotics Anonymous. Until then I had remained in recovery and abstinent from all drugs for 4 years and 6 months. My mental health started to deteriorate with massive bouts of depression and suicide attempts. I couldn't face my colleagues in work. At that time, I was working as a substance misuse worker for a charity in Merseyside. I isolated myself from society and shortly afterwards was also diagnosed with meningitis, hepatitis and PTSD. Shortly after my relapse I found a dear friend dead in my home. My world became one crisis after another. I began seeing and hearing things which weren't there and reported it to my doctor, until eventually a loved one contacted the mental health team to have me sectioned under the Mental Health Act. Unfortunately, I became paranoid and refused help and believed

149

people were out to get me, I drank and used substances to block out the trauma and things I believed I was seeing. I really believed my life was about to end and couldn't cope and eventually I was evicted from my home, the home I had lived in for 3 years, losing all my property. I really have no idea why I committed this crime. I just remember walking around my home in fear and screaming out in despair most days. I cannot I feel ever put right the hurt my victims feel but can make the effort to make amends which I am sincere in making. I deserve and accept the consequences of my actions and my plea is guilty. This letter to you is about a traumatic life experience I went through and by no means a way of justifying my behaviour. I just know I swore to myself and gave promise to many that I would never return to active addiction again. For that I was wrong as having cancer and my mortality at question terrified me to the point that I lost my mind! To this day I still shudder at the consequences and impact of my actions on the lives of innocent people. I only hope and pray that I can continue to someday be the man I can be as I have had enough of drugs and active addiction and only wish to help the society I live in. I am in no way the habitual criminal I once was in society and believe the traumatic series of events contributed massively to my current predicament causing the impact I have had on my community. I am now in remission from cancer and back in my own personal recovery and hope never to be in a court ever again. I have a deep sense of remorse and a sincere desire to make redress for my actions, and I am willing to face the victims of my crime, one day if possible, to put right the wrongs I have caused. If your honour could somehow arrange for me to compensate them alongside sentencing today I would be grateful for that opportunity. It is therefore with solemn regret that I throw myself at the mercy of the court and ask only that these mitigating circumstances be considered in regards of sentencing.

Mr William Moore

Judge Foster looked over the rim of his glasses and stared straight at me. He didn't speak directly to me but to my counsel, muttering a few words to her about the three-strike law, and then turned towards me.

'Well, Mr Moore, as you have a long history of criminality you will receive a custodial sentence and having taken into account the twenty-five per cent discount for your guilty plea, I am sentencing you today to serve 876 days.' Then he added, 'I hope that you take this opportunity to reflect on your actions.'

Reflect? I had been in constant anxiety for almost five months *reflecting*. I was in shock. What purpose would sending me to prison achieve? I felt the injustice of it but the outcome was inevitably out of my hands. However, I had broken into my neighbour's house and stolen items not belonging to me and these were the consequences. Why I did what I did still confuses me. It was wrong and with a sounder, clearer mind I understood that. But such insight had come far too late to save me.

'A7853AP Moore, welcome back to the big house. It's been a while,' said the old prison officer on the reception desk. 'Plenty of cockroaches for company,' he said as I walked away to be searched.

'OK, you know the drill: strip in there and put your clothes in the box to be scanned.'

I recognised the old-school screw from many years earlier. Sixteen years might have passed since I was last in HMP Liverpool but some of the same old faces remained – still serving their sentences. I finished stripping and stood in front of the officer wearing only a blue towel that covered my private parts.

'OK, sit in that chair,' he said pointing to a grey, solid chair with the words 'Big Boss' written on it. This was a chair that had a metal detector embedded within it. I positioned myself on the chair and heard a beep, jumping up I looked behind me. 'What's that?' I asked.

'You haven't got a phone up there, have you?' the screw said, shaking his head and looking disappointed.

'Nope, not me, guv.'

'Try it again. Take another seat.'

This time the seat didn't beep, and I was ushered through to the healthcare department. I answered a few basic questions, saying 'no' to all of them. I've always been comfortable in front of a camera but here in the prison reception my vanity had been replaced by deep shame.

I was given a plate of cold chips, mushy peas and a fish of sorts; I didn't have much of an appetite and waited until my name was called.

'Moore A7853AP,' shouted an elderly female officer with a kind face and a warm smile. 'How are you feeling?' she asked as she showed me into a plastic-partitioned cubicle and told me to take a seat in front of a wooden table.

'OK, just a few questions. Nothing to worry about,' she said. 'Can you confirm your date of birth?'

I knew the questions were routine: Was I feeling suicidal? Did I require a special diet or a smoker's pack? The latter consisted of a vape pen – gone were the days when prisoners could smoke tobacco. For those that didn't smoke, you could get a sweet pack: a packet of custard creams, a Mars Bar, a bottle of orange juice and a packet of Polos. I answered in the negative to nearly all her questions but yes to the sweet pack.

'OK. Finally, would you like a phone call to let anyone know you're here?' she asked, smiling as she finished typing away on her computer.

'Yes, please. I'd like to call my mum to let her know I'm OK,' I said, depressed at the thought of having to tell my poor mother that I was in prison once again.

She led me to a pin phone and dialled the access digits. She gave me two minutes to speak with my mum. Any more would have broken my heart so I was fine with the limitation. Not that I had a choice – from now on everything in my life would be controlled by the prison service.

Mum answered the phone straightaway. She was worried but confident I was going to be OK, told me to stay safe and to remember to pray every day. My mum was a devout Catholic and believed God was good and that he'd put me in prison for a reason. I didn't share her opinion and thought he was an arse, but that wasn't something I needed to tell her just then. She told me she loved me and that she would visit me soon.

I walked away from the phone call and sat in the waiting room for another hour with only my thoughts for company. It was a far cry from when I was last here and calling my mum to beg for money so I could buy drugs. I remember, after going through yet another horrendous withdrawal and feeling raw and emotional, that I told her I loved her. She couldn't even bring herself to reciprocate the love I desperately craved back then. It would tear my soul apart, sitting alone in my cell each evening with my head in my hands, sobbing for the love of the woman who brought me into this world and nurtured me the best she could. I understood now why she took a step back in those days as I was full of empty promises, giving her and my family false hope every time I was locked up because of my drug use. Drug addicts back then didn't have the intervention we have these days, so I was on that never-ending cycle of prisons, institutions and near death.

On reflection, the call I'd just had with my mum was loving and caring and how it should've been all those years ago. We forget what we put our loved ones through: they too have to serve a sentence, not in an actual prison but imprisoned in a mind full of fear. My mum used to tell me she'd pray to God every night to have me locked up.

It was the only time she could find any solace or peace, but it was always a brief interlude. The thought of the knock on the door from the police to say her son was dead would have her panicking, the phone ringing caused her massive anxiety, the unknown had her in constant fear. I once got arrested and gave the police my brother's details instead of my own because I was on their wanted list. While in the cell, I swallowed a load of tablets I had concealed in my sock, not thinking of the consequences. The next thing I remember was waking up in the intensive care unit at the Royal University Hospital in Liverpool. My mum was standing over the bed, while two police officers stood guard on the other side of the door.

'Are you OK, son?' she had said with tears streaming down her face. She had taken hold of my hand, tightly squeezing it while rubbing my forehead with a damp cloth.

'They don't know who I am do they, Mum?' I said, looking towards the door at the two police officers.

'I had to tell them who you really were, son. You've been in a coma for almost a week,' she said sobbing.

'You are messing. What the fuck! They're going to put me away now,' I said, my face screwed up in anger. The drugs turned me into a monster – a selfish, horrible monster. All I could think about was myself and not what I had put my mother through. When she had got the call from the hospital to tell her that her son, Tony, was in a coma, she didn't know what to think. She told me later she believed Tony had been injured while on tour with the British Army in Iraq and was shocked to see me on that bed because of an overdose. That day someone up there was looking down on me, because my mother telling the police who I really was changed my life for the better.

Chapter 18
Prison

Not mine own fears, nor the prophetic soul
Of the wide world dreaming on things to come,
Can yet the lease of my true love control,
Supposed as forfeit to a confin'd doom.

Sonnet CVII,
William Shakespeare

I DRAGGED my plastic bag of possessions behind me as the officer walked me along the corridor to the new arrival cells on A wing. Under my arm I had two standard green sheets and a small towel. They had all seen better days but at least they smelled reasonably clean. The industrial washing machines and dryers of the prison laundries were big enough to accommodate a man. I found out later that the previous week they had, and the unfortunate occupant was still recovering on the hospital wing.

At least for the first one or two nights I could expect to be allocated a single cell, giving me time to gather my thoughts and come to terms with settling into my new home for the next couple of years. The officer unlocked the cell door and as soon as I had stepped in the door slammed behind me. The first thing to hit me was the smell. Feet, tobacco smoke, stagnant water and a filthy toilet. The only light came from the overhead, dim nightlight and the flicker of a muted TV screen. I found the light switch and the cell was flooded with a harsh white fluorescent light. I took in the missing toilet door; two formerly white, now yellow-grey plastic tubs which I only realised later were meant to be chairs; the barred window partly exposed to the elements, its Perspex panes long smashed. The rickety-looking table was strewn with a hideous mess of used teabags, half-eaten food scraps and dimps – the tiny remains of hand-rolled cigarettes. There was a two-tier bunk: on the top bunk lay a bare plastic mattress and, on the lower, a bundle of filthy bedsheets and blankets. The squalor, the graffiti-covered walls, the general air of resentment were almost as bad as my three-year hell in Thailand. As I stood in the cell trying to take it all in I jumped back, startled. The heap of bedclothes on the bottom bunk was moving and a grunting noise emanating from within.

Oh, for fuck's sake! I had a pad-mate. The slumbering form made a couple of attempts to raise himself upright, then gave up and fell back into the heap. He peered at me horizontally.

'Me you OK, yes?' in a thick Eastern European accent was all he could manage before a fit of cackling overtook him, closely followed by a hacking cough. The putrid smell coming from his diseased innards as he coughed up flecks of phlegm practically knocked me out. The guy was completely out of it. I didn't know for sure on what drug, but I guessed it was spice.

Bollocks to this, I thought, and jammed my thumb on the emergency buzzer. This would sound an alarm in the wing screws' office. I knew from past experience that the time taken to answer could range from a couple of minutes to well over an hour. On this occasion I was in luck: the door opened again after only a minute or so. I had worked myself up into an indignant temper and was ready to kick off. There was no need. The officer put his hand up in a 'calm down' gesture and beckoned me to follow. I was deposited in another cell, no better in what it had to offer in terms of comforts, but at least it was empty and not in such a state of absolute squalor.

The officer, a Mr Moon who had been allocated to me as my keyworker, told me he had been reading up on me on the prison system NOMS [National Offender Management Service] database as the buzzer sounded. Although I had tried to keep out of trouble in the past, I had gained a reputation for getting myself in it. And when I did, it was well documented on their database that I could be – as Mr Moon told me – 'a bit of a handful'.

As I lay down to sleep on that first night alone with my thoughts, the memories came flooding back. Of sharing an overcrowded cell with up to eighty other inmates in horrendous conditions when I was in Klong Prem prison in Bangkok, after I had been moved from Chiang Mai. In Klong Prem, there was no bell to press. You tried to sleep on the hard, unrelenting, concrete floor while in a state of perpetual alert – sharing a cell full of drug-crazed junkies who held the sanctity of life in contempt. The cells were full of cockroaches, bedbugs and mosquitoes that were attracted to the heat of the mass of sweaty bodies lying desperately on top of one another.

When the cell door was locked for the night, I would routinely witness gang rapes and vicious beatings. On more than one occasion I woke to find a lifeless hanging body – the tongue obscenely protruding from a blackened face. I remember thinking that I was probably going to die at the hands of the tattooed Thai gangs or acquire a fatal disease like AIDS or hepatitis. Either way, I was never going to get out of there alive.

The cramped conditions, the nightly screams and the sickly stench of rotting flesh in the intense heat soon became the norm. The chronic masturbators were the worst, constantly renting pornography magazines and waiting in line to toss themselves off in full view of everyone, like they were on the main stage in Glastonbury, without shame or a care in the world for those of us who were forced to spectate.

So here I was on A wing and perhaps, on reflection, I could acknowledge how comparatively lucky I was. I finally managed to get some sleep.

Three weeks have passed and I'm getting really angry. I've been waiting ten days for an appointment with the doctor; my left ear feels like I've got a constant riot bell kicking off inside it. Everything is testing my patience. Twenty-three hours banged up every day, bedsores, mental isolation, pure madness, no exercise routine and no sunshine for vitamin D. 'Walton is a SHITHOLE,' I scream, frustrated with the lack of care bordering on outright neglect.

'I'll sort it later, son.' 'It'll have to be tomorrow now.' 'Definitely next week.' 'I'll make sure you get it when you're out.' My needs were constantly dismissed.

The only officer who had been helpful and supportive was Mr Moon. He made time each week to sit me down and have a chat. The prison was in a state of chaos and the management seemed to have completely lost control. Some staff seemed to mean well but hadn't got a clue and were brand new out of the box. Maintenance was all but non-existent. Bare wires, blocked drains and toilets are the norm. Senior staff – sometimes officers with twenty-to-thirty-year careers – were clearly resigned to having lost the war on drugs, the endemic violence and squalid conditions. The healthcare system was hopeless – even my history of mental health and physical illness failed to get me the treatment I really needed.

Thailand had been better in the sense of more freedom. There were many differences and both prison systems had their flaws, but at least you were out of your cell all day and mixing with other inmates. Not shacked up for long periods of time with nothing but your own thoughts for company. That way madness lies.

I saw addiction run riot, vapes, tablets, tobacco. Walton prison seemed to be touting drugs, mainly spice, to the most vulnerable of inmates. People were at cell doors blatantly (and unforgivably) selling anything and everything for just one more hit. But it never is just one more – I'll repeat, one is too many and a thousand never enough – but here on the landings everything must go. Inmates trying to sell their meals – 'Hey, mate, you can have my roasties,' 'I've got a boss chicken here. Honest, it's a belter,' 'What about my trackies and trainers?' 'Fuck it, man, you can have my soul' – were the everyday shouts on the wing; it was sad to see addicts losing themselves in the system for just one more . . .

Debt is endemic in prison establishments. It happens all over the world.

Air was an overweight Thai – covered head to toe in tattoos. He was an ex-boxer and the head honcho of his gang in Chiang Mai Central Prison. I had borrowed a couple of items from him, a couple of packets of Krong Thip Thai cigarettes and a pack of Ovaltine the week before, which I used to purchase my daily dose of tramadol painkillers. I had managed to pay back the bulk of the debt, which was the cigarettes, leaving myself as usual with nothing. Unfortunately, I was short and I still owed him, although I was sure he'd wait until Kathleen the missionary came to visit. That way I could pay him in full but I would probably end up owing him again – a vicious circle as we wallowed in an everlasting quicksand of debt.

'Yo farang, you Ovanteen na? You pay me now!' Air demanded as I walked out of the boxing compound after a long afternoon's workout on the bags and pads. Jom, a pretty ladyboy, was standing protected behind the visitors' gate, smiling and waving towards me, making me feel uncomfortable with her shouts of 'Yoo-hoo, Billy. You OK na?' Secretly I was flattered by the attention. Air noticed this and I believe felt threatened in some strange way. He felt it was important to humiliate me for no reason other than jealousy. I smiled and half-heartedly waved back at Jom and then blushed as she blew me a kiss, hearing raucous laughter from Air and his gang.

'You hear me, farang, you pay me Ovanteen now na,' spat Air aggressively.

'Next week,' I quickly snapped back.

Air was 'performing' in front of his boys; he knew I always paid my debts. Jom looked at both of us then mouthed the words 'Go now.' *Fuck that*, I thought. I wasn't letting this fat fuck give me a hard time.

He slowly and purposefully walked towards me with about eight of his gang members in tow. He stood in front while they spread out in a semi-circle behind him, making themselves look more threatening. He stopped with an open palm circling a closed fist, a subtle warning that said do as you're told or we will beat the shit out of you.

'Look, Air, I'll pay next week. You know I will,' I told him as calmly and as politely as possible. The last thing I wanted was to be involved in a fight.

'Ari I-heeya, ow dop nar mii?' ('Fucking buffalo, do you want me to slap your face?') Air boomed, showing me the back of his hand and then feigning a bitch slap that had me flinching. My temper was bubbling as Air mocked me in front of his friends while Jom looked on. His gang again laughed and shouted something in Thai that I didn't understand. The sweat was pouring down my face and my heart began to pump ferociously. I knew what was coming next. I had a choice – the primal fight or flight.

I glanced briefly at Jom, her pretty face a mask of fright as she mouthed the word 'RUN.'

I smiled back, looked directly at Air and threw a right cross, landing it squarely on his nose, rocking him on his feet. He stumbled back into the hands of his gang, who all looked on in shocked horror. Everything seemed to happen in slow motion as I watched and admired my handiwork before snapping out of it. I turned quickly on my heels and ran as fast as I could in the direction of the commander's quarters before the gang annihilated me. I heard the yells and screams of the angry mob baying for my blood. They were close on my heels.

'Fuck, fuck, fuck,' I muttered to no one in particular.

Suddenly a couple of gang members appeared in front of me from nowhere. *Shit!* I was only yards from safety.

I stopped, doubling over, hands on knees and struggling to breathe. I looked around for another escape route but there was nothing. Air and his gang were closing fast. A hand reached for my throat and my arms were pinned behind my back by at least two others. At that moment, Ali the Iranian came running towards us screaming,

'Yo, stop my friends. This is stupid. Nobody needs to get hurt,' Ali said, pleading with the crowd who had gathered. Despite my arms being wrenched behind me, my fists were clenched tight, ready to fight a losing battle, but ready anyway. Ali spoke to Air, who then looked towards me and nodded. Ali approached and told me if I could pay the debt in double immediately then Air would be prepared to let it go this time. I would have paid more than double at that moment. I was grateful to Ali for his intervention, but I was also surprised as we had history, and a violent one at that. Although we never became the best of friends, Ali and I regarded each other with mutual respect during our remaining time in Chiang Mai prison.

★ ★ ★

Miss D, the head cleaning officer on Liverpool's A wing, was someone you didn't mess with and someone who had worked in the prison system for years. Her depth of experience meant she knew every trick in the book. You couldn't get anything past her. If she thought you were taking the piss you would certainly know about it; she was both loved and hated at the same time and most new inmates didn't know how to take her.

She was tall for a woman, middle-aged, and had her blonde hair in a ponytail that perched on the top of her head. She was always screaming and shouting at some rag-arse for taking the piss. It was her job to maintain order and control, and she did it well. If you wanted a decent job and the chance to get out of your cell, then Miss D was the one you applied to.

I'd asked her for a job three weeks earlier when I first arrived and resented the fact that I was still banged up twenty-three hours a day. As things were, I would have rather been in a Thai jail.

'Hey, Moore, you still after a cleaner's job?' Miss D asked me one afternoon while I was heading down the stairs for my evening meal.

'Yes, I'd love one, Miss.'

She looked at me enquiringly. 'Do you like the gym?' she asked, looking me up and down, knowing from my bulky physique that I obviously did.

'Er, yeah, but I'm not a big fan of the gym these days,' I lied.

It was definitely a trick question. Matt, one of the inmates who worked as a cleaner, had warned me about how to answer any questions she might ask. 'Miss D hates her cleaners using the job to get more gym privileges,' Big Matt told me when I first landed on the wing.

'So, if I give you a job, don't take the piss and go to the gym unless I say so. Do you understand me?' she said, pointing her finger at me. For some reason I felt like a school kid getting told off.

'Of course, miss. No gym.' I would have said anything to get out of my cell and could live without training for a while.

Over time I got to know Miss D and saw through the tough exterior to a beautiful soul and a big heart. She sat with me for over an hour one morning while we waited for healthcare to check on me. I wasn't feeling too good and my anxiety was through the roof, my ears were killing me and I was suffering with terrible headaches to a point where I'd convinced myself I was having a stroke. Miss D just sat there and told me not to worry and that I was going to be fine, while muttering under her breath what a bunch of twats healthcare were for the delay in attending an emergency.

Chapter 19

Clean

Hope is a lover's staff; walk hence with that
And manage it against despairing thoughts.

The Two Gentlemen of Verona Act 3, Scene 1,
William Shakespeare

JUST as debt is endemic in prison, so are drugs. Liverpool prison's drug problem has become an epidemic. Virtually all drugs are available but the worst of them all is spice. Supposedly a synthetic substitute for cannabis that could evade traditional drug detection, spice is a noxious chemical manufactured in laboratories with widespread indifference towards how unpredictable its effects can be. It can produce a zombie-like effect on one user while another can become violent, even psychotic. It is smuggled into prisons in many ingenious ways: inmates get friends, partners and families to dip a piece of A4 paper into spice liquid, then once it has dried write a loving letter on it that passes through the prison censors. The drug-impregnated letter is now worth £200 on the prison landings. The paper is carefully torn into strips and smoked in a variety of ways. Some inmates use vapes, others mix it with tobacco – when they can get it on the prison black market – but the most common process is to mix it with teabags and bible paper. The results can be catastrophic. The mindset among users is that every hour spent out of their heads is an hour less spent in the jail.

I got talking to Red, an orderly, and Mac, a biohazard cleaner, who worked in the segregation unit known as the Block located on the lowest dungeon level of the prison wings. I was curious to find out why Mac seemed to be always down there, clad head to toe in white overalls – the sort you see worn by forensic scientists on TV crime dramas. My stomach heaved when I found out he was regularly called upon to clean up after 'dirty protests'. Prisoners put into the segregation cells would smear their shit all over the walls, the insane reasoning being that by protesting in this way, they would get themselves moved back into the main cell blocks. Of course, if this did happen, other prisoners would find out and attack the protesters for their stomach-churning behaviour – so back they would go to the seg unit for their own safety. Mac could talk you into a coma with his detailed descriptions of cleaning up filthy cells with power washers and the disposal of soiled bedding and mattresses into incineration and biohazard bags.

Prison mattresses and pillows bear little resemblance to the well-sprung and soft comfort of their equivalents at home. Prison varieties are made from plastic foam covered in sleeves of blue vinyl, impregnated, during manufacture, with a bactericide. Despite all being made of exactly the same stuff, mattresses and pillows have bewilderingly different properties. A brand-new standard-issue prison mattress – about four inches thick and specially cut in length to be either just too long or just too short for the iron bedsteads – is brutally unforgiving. On first use, it is a bit like lying on a concrete floor. Miraculously, by the following morning the mattress has gained a deep body-shaped indentation along the middle section of its length and there it stays. No amount of pummelling makes any difference and it remains that way throughout your stay. The pillow, on the other hand, despite its identical construction, performs in an entirely different manner. Within microseconds of raising your head any minor impression made on the unforgiving foam quickly disappears and the pillow immediately restores itself to the comfort and shape of a concrete breeze block.

One of the reasons touted for the manufacturing specifications of all prison cell furnishing – from sheets to rickety tables and bolted-down iron beds – is safety and fire resistance. Anything sharp has been vetoed from supplied items, and the pillows, mattresses and fabrics liberally treated with fire-resistant chemicals. Just as the dirty protesters have their horrible habit of fouling their own living space, the arsonists are known to frequently set fire to the inside of their own locked cells. Their 'cry for help' of mental anguish is swiftly overtaken by real cries of alarm as the flames and dangers of smoke inhalation take hold.

These demonstrations tend to take place during the long evening and night hours, when staff numbers are at their lowest. As the 'rules of engagement' with prisoners prohibit staff opening cell doors unless they are in sufficient numbers, the prison management has, over the years, devised an ingenious solution. Each reinforced metal cell door is fitted with a small, chest-high aperture – about the diameter of an aerosol cap – with a simple flap. On discovery of a cell fire, the night officer jams the high-pressure fire hose into the opening and releases the valve until help arrives. The ensuing torrent of water, forced through a carefully designed outlet on the end of the hose, forms an all-enveloping spray designed to extinguish the fire. The volume of water released can be quite dramatic. While the self-harming inmate can be rescued from his endeavours to end his time through smoke and fire, there have been occasions when a no-less unpleasant death through drowning has been a near result.

While most arsonists, in prisons at least, keep their fire-raising to themselves, this is not always the case. I remember one tragic case many years before while in Stafford prison when a guy was woken from his drug-induced stupor to find his shared cell thick with smoke and fire coming from the toilet area. His cellmate had lost the plot and decided to end his life and, in choosing to do so, killed them both. As the fire took hold, we were rushed out of our cells as the whole wing was evacuated to the sports field. We watched in horror as a helicopter landed on the prison exercise yard and emergency services as well as prison officers fought in vain to save the lives of the two men trapped in their burning coffin.

Sadly, issues of mental health and the ability of the prison system to cope sometimes boil over into unacceptable and distressing events. Red told me of another occasion when a young lad, barely in his twenties, had over time been giving the staff verbal abuse and physical aggro. A small group of screws disabled the security cameras covering the seg unit and, unlocking his cell door, told him he could take some exercise. The reality was he was beaten to a pulp and had all his top front teeth knocked out. Later, Red and Mac, in his biohazard suit, were given a £5 bonus on their prison wages to clean up the blood and broken teeth. The perpetrators were, of course, never held to account. Their victim was far too frightened to complain.

During my time in various prisons and on many occasions, I too had been thrown into isolation from the rest of the prison population. The worst was when I was in Chiang Mai Central Prison. I'd had an altercation with one of the other foreign inmates, a guy called Scott, over a couple of tramadol painkillers. The argument got heated and I reacted in the only way I knew how – with my fists. In fairness, Scott had fought back hard, but I had the better of him and caught him with about a dozen kidney blows that caused him to collapse in a heap, struggling to breathe. Meanwhile, an older Italian inmate blew the cell whistle to raise the alarm. The guards came running in numbers along with half-a-dozen trusted inmates (blue shirts) and they collectively dragged me off Scott.

'Ari farang, I heeya?' ('What are you doing, you animal?') one shouted, just before smashing me across the back of the head with his baton, knocking me out cold. I awoke not long after in the courtyard with the guards and trustees circling me – all the time spitting out abuse in rapid Thai that I couldn't understand. Prisit, the head commando, who had saved me on many occasions, walked over shaking his head with a disappointed look.

'Mr Billy, this time you have gone too far, you will be punished severely for this,' he said, shaking his head in disgust.

My protests fell on deaf ears as he ordered a couple of trustees to put shackles around my ankles and send me to 'hong soi' – a three-foot-wide and four-foot-high punishment cell under the stairway of one of the cell blocks. These kinds of punishments were feared by everyone: the stifling heat, the horrendous isolation, the darkness swarming with bugs, and the only way to sleep in a foetal position on the hard, unforgiving, concrete floor. I spent a whole week in these tortuous conditions being fed through a small hatch twice a day on a diet of sticky rice and soup that crawled with maggots and flies. I would have swapped the loss of my teeth for one day out of there. Even a short stay and I swear I was going to lose my mind for good.

Miss D stopped me one morning while I was mopping the landing, 'Morning, lid, how are you feeling?' she asked ('lid' coming from rhyming slang for 'our kid'). 'You've been in and out of these places all your life, haven't you, Billy? I mean it's a different story this time, the cancer, the drugs, you've had it tough haven't you, kidder?' It was said with compassion and I could only look at the floor to hide my shame. I was embarrassed. In fact, I felt horrendous.

'I understand that under normal circumstances you wouldn't be robbing your neighbour's jewellery in a pair of flip-flops and your underpants at three o'clock in the morning, lid,' she laughed, trying to lighten the mood. 'It was the drugs, that's clear. It's terrible what it does to some of these young kids who keep coming in and out of here. No way to live, hey?' she said as she looked over the landing at some of the young inmates running around, obviously up to no good, trying to score their daily fix.

I was allocated a job in the Welcome Centre. There was nothing fucking *welcoming* about it. However, it meant I was to stay on A wing, which although grim wasn't in the grip of the gangs that ruled the roost on some of the other wings. My role consisted of giving each new intake during the induction a down-to-earth talk and friendly advice on dealing with prison life. It was a great way for me to reach out to just that one person, to maybe give them a sliver of hope. To let them know there's a better way of living other than coming in and out of prison for the rest of their lives or dying in the grip of addiction or at the hands of some gang member.

'Hello, my name's Billy. Welcome to hell! Is there anyone who hasn't been to prison before?' I would ask the motley crew of newcomers plus, of course, a few familiar faces back again after learning absolutely nothing from the last time they were here.

As a couple of hands shot up, I'd focus my attention on them, looking into each of their faces, seeing myself many years before when I first came to prison. All I remember was being absolutely terrified of the unknown, but manly pride made me determined to mask my fear.

I'd said this spiel a hundred times or more while at Walton prison as it was my role to provide information. I knew most of what I said would fall on deaf ears and couldn't expect any miracles. I knew from experience the only way to get through to someone is to say it how it is, no holds barred. This was prison, not some fuckin' kindergarten.

'First things first. Do not get yourself in debt – the interest rates in here are high,' I warned them. 'Don't share other people's vapes. You never know, it could be contaminated with spice and you'll only know it when you're knocking on someone's door in a pair of Ugg boots trying to sell them a plate of roasties with your head smashed in.' That usually gets a laugh from the regulars while the newcomers just look on in shock. I tell them that here in Walton prison two people have died in under a week, both from using spice.

Heroin, cannabis, cocaine, EES, spice . . . drugs are fucking everywhere, and I am angry and wrapped up in uncomfortable feelings. My relationship is falling apart, it has been for a while and I am banged up in here and there is nothing I can do about it.

Thoughts of using flow through my mind, the temptation is there on the landing just a few cells away. My disease is very cunning and insidious, people, places and things are very difficult to avoid while in prison. It scares me. I'm almost eight months clean, in recovery, and the days can be dark and lonely and the temptation almost overwhelming.

'Just one,' it whispers, but it's never just one. My only chance of surviving is not to pick up that first drug, no matter what. Come hell or high water, the only answer is, 'Just don't use.' But is it enough? *NO MATTER WHAT?*

I find myself answering the call, 'Yo, Billy. 'Ere, lad, get on this. My pad-mate's got a major parcel, bro.' Tommo was whispering loudly through the gap in the side of the grey steel door. 'Pure Bobby, lad. Who has the graft on here?' he asked, as if I knew or wanted to know.

'I'm not sure, mate,' I replied, feeling uncomfortable.

'Get on it, bro. I'll have a goodie bag sorted for you soon, Billy,' he whispered through the gap of the door.

'I DON'T TAKE DRUGS!' I shouted, surprising myself. I needed him to know I didn't want anything, but my inner demons were alive and screaming. My palms felt sweaty. I knew if I used, I'd be back on the roof or Sellotaped to the drug hatch. One day, one hour, one minute.

'Hold on tight,' I kept repeating to myself. 'Just don't use!'

Chapter 20

Malaise

When a wise man gives thee better counsel, give me mine again.
I would have none but knaves follow it, since a fool gives it.

King Lear Act 2, Scene 4,
William Shakespeare

A LETTER arrived from my friend Colin, who lived in East Ayrshire. In it was a poem he had written.

I have deep fears of not being enough so went to therapy to call my bluff. An inconsistent maze of thoughts which brings me down and makes me frown, my thinking was adjourned with golden brown, it had me up it had me down.

The therapist says I'll soon be free, in control and ready to roll. Advising me to abstain from mood-altering drugs and binge on tonic water, claps and hugs.

Confused with emotions and a racing mind but advised to accept my feelings and explore the thoughts, expand my brain with what they find.

And yes, I understand self-empower, that's what Charlie did for £60 an hour, as I was feeling supersonic, I've been analysed and diagnosed with a disease which is chronic.

The counsellor tells me to love myself and it will all be fine, I say at least seduce me over a glass of wine.

I'm vulnerable here as you see, this isn't who I am, what you hear or what I see, my life's been strange full of twists and turns, a rollercoaster spent in a chemical toaster.

A psychic change from acting out is replaced by terror, fears and doubts, feelings of euphoria replaced by sadness while letting go of self-made madness.

In charge of my own demise, I'll wilt or grow before your eyes, the key holder of my own success and the instigator of all the mess. Wisdom is the key to set me free. I'm not who I think I am. Or what I see.

Reading the poem grounded me. It helped me realise that I wasn't alone; that people out there cared and understood because they too had once been in a dark place. I had friends on the outside who were there for me and I felt gratitude for the support I had in my life. If I was in addiction and using drugs like I had done during every other sentence, then I would be sitting here alone, wallowing in self-pity, resenting myself and everyone around me. So, it was letters like this that reminded me of how fortunate I was. Life wasn't all bad when you looked at the bigger picture. I also reminded myself that things had been worse in my life, a lot worse.

Ste the E, an approval-seeking drug lord, can't do his bang up. The nickname came from his clubland days when he was involved in huge overseas drug deals involving Ecstasy tablets. He is in the next cell to me and hammers impatiently on his door every dinner time.

'Boss! Boss!' he screams. 'I think you might have forgot to open me up for work,' he shouts, fearing he'd have to spend the rest of the afternoon in his cell. Always thinking about himself and his hidden millions. Millions he can't spend banged up in Walton.

I had read his depositions and learned Ste had talked himself into a fifteen-year sentence when the police bugged his white BMW 5. He was small and well-built with solid shoulders and cropped fair hair that was quickly receding. He told me he was a massive steroid abuser and that when he was in his youth he had a body that belonged in muscle mags. He wore a sheepskin coat that looked like it was borrowed from the costume department of *Only Fools and Horses* and explained that, when he was arrested, he was classed as a *high-risk* inmate and placed on the escape list. I didn't doubt any of what he told me was true, but he loved the status and revelled in the opportunity to lecture you. I guess he felt the need to feel important as well as dangerous but he was just another imprisoned drug dealer at the end of the day.

He's been in two years and his cell resembles a bombsite. It reeks of tuna with half-eaten tins strewn everywhere; self-care long gone, as well as his mind. The Gaza Strip would look like paradise in comparison and a Thailand shit pit would smell better. Hygiene is not one of his strong points.

'I'm a millionaire,' he constantly pecks. 'What's happing, smiler? Here he is. How's the breath, Robbo?' he shouts down the landing.

'Not as bad as your pad, Del Boy. It fucking stinks and sort that sheepie out, ya scruff,' Robbo shouts back.

The banter is constant but underneath it is an element of truth. Robbo's breath does stink and Ste the E's pad is a shithole. I look around and laugh. It's the banter that gets some people through the day.

Ste stands next to me, telling me one of his stories. They are all the same: money, champagne and the kilos of cocaine and Ecstasy.

'Did I ever tell you the story about the Bombay mafia?' Ste begins and waffles on about the big jobs he's done in the past. Curtis Warren, the Colombian cartel . . . I've heard it a thousand times and if he isn't telling me he's telling someone else. Yet, it always has a different ending. Ste had a few quid years, I don't doubt that, but now he's broke and never has the humility to admit it. There's no one in here to impress and he behaves like an arrogant narcissist that stinks of piss.

'Here I am, big hitter, bam bam,' he shouts while shadow boxing along the landing. 'When the right hand lands, you'll know about it,' he grunts between punches at no one in particular.

His head's gone; it's obvious he's not the full ticket and he doesn't even know it. The ultimate narcissist. Who-the-fuck-wants-to-be-a-millionaire is really annoying me and everyone he comes into contact with. Even the prison chaplaincy avoids him, and that's saying something, because they are the most non-judgemental people in here.

'I'm clever me, lad, I've got a calculator memory,' he boasts. Pity he can't remember his own porkies. I have to bite my tongue and tolerate his constant repetitive shite.

Ste's really getting on my nerves today. I ask him whether I can borrow his toaster – he is my neighbour after all and the only inmate to possess one on our wing.

'I'm using it!' he responds aggressively.

'Look, we're getting banged up now. I'll only be five minutes,' I say, trying to keep my cool. It isn't the first time I've asked to use it, so I'm a little bit taken aback by his abruptness. There's never been a problem before.

'I'm using it,' he snarls again, eyes bulging and spittle flying in my direction.

I've had enough of his attitude. It isn't what he said to me, it's the tone it is delivered in that is pissing me off.

I walk towards him and without hesitation push him into his cell, shut the door and clench my fists, ready to smash his head in. I wouldn't speak to myself like that never mind this ballbag and his shed of a toaster.

'Let's go for it, I'm fed up of your attitude,' I growl, preparing to throw a punch. This is the first time since I've come away that I've lost it to a point I am ready to fight and lose any privileges I'm entitled to.

'Er, I'm not losing my job because of you and I've got my appeal and Cat D to consider,' he splutters, his eyes full of panic as he looks over my shoulder at the closed door behind me, blocking his escape route.

I can see he's backing down and to be honest I don't want to be trading blows. We both probably have our own shit going on and now I feel badly about over-reacting. He's lucky I can rein in my temper these days, because years, even months ago, we would have been rolling around scrapping on the floor. So, with my newfound wisdom and maturity, I get a grip on myself.

'Sorry, lad, I just saw red for a moment there,' I say in a soft voice. Ste quickly regains his composure and immediately puts on a front to hide his shame, finding the courage to respond with some crazy shit about seeing me on the outside in eight years. I smile to myself and walk away. Threats spoken behind prison bars soon lose their charm.

I know that my pride can be dangerous in a place like this; someone has to back down or you might *not* live to fight another day. I take it on the chin and let him rant. It'll probably make him feel better to see me walk away.

Tony had a head that belonged on a beluga whale and slobbered every time he laughed – which was pretty much all the time. He'd been in and out of prison for most of his life and was one of many with mental health problems who had been failed by the prison system. Another lost and forgotten soul. Tony was known by all the staff as a likeable nuisance, but he was a pain in the arse for the lads on A wing, always kicking off and in need of attention. The alarm would be raised, the screws would come in force, while he stood there laughing and screaming, his grey prison jumper covered in gravy stains and slobber. This would happen daily, kicking off, smashing his cell up and flooding the whole wing. He was constantly getting banged up or taken down to the segregation unit where you could hear him laughing manically.

Ste the E also thought he was a top counsellor; he was the A-wing listener. I doubted he listened to anything but his own ego and fairy tales these days.

'Here I am. I'll sort it out, boss, just leave it with me,' Ste said, waving his hand in the air and offering to have a chat with Tony after yet another drama. Ste just loved licking arse, anything for a few brownie points. He was big on blowing his own trumpet too and telling anyone who would listen about the many lives he had saved since becoming a listener, which was basically an inmate trained by the Samaritans to listen and signpost vulnerable inmates who were finding it difficult to cope with prison life. Ste thought he was the dog's bollocks and that after having a little chat about life and God with him, you would be happy as Larry, filled with joy and free again. He was deluded. He was not only the listener, he had about a dozen other self-awarded titles. His skillset was endless and about the only thing missing was his superhero cape.

'Yeah, Tony needs someone who's sensible and knows what he's talking about,' he said, looking in our direction and shaking his head, like we were all thick and couldn't string a sentence together. I knew it was a personal dig at me. I sensed he felt inadequate, even intimidated, when he was in my company. He reminded me of Russell Brand, throwing big words together in his conversations, save that he made no sense at all.

Robbo laughed. 'Fuckin' hell, he'll be on a suicide watch after speaking to you.' The rest of the wing cleaners burst into fits of laughter. 'Tell him about the palm trees and Olympic-size swimming pool that you own, Ste,' Robbo continued with the banter.

'They're all jealous. Tony, come over here, lad. I'll talk to you. Tell us what's bothering you,' we heard him say as he dismissed Robbo's comments.

The one thing I liked about Ste, regardless of his massive ego, narcissistic personality and lick-arse behaviour, was the way he played the system. He had a certain level of intellect and was the only inmate in the prison with access to all areas. He was called a grass shithouse but never reacted, he just let it go over his head, which annoyed most people who came across him.

'If you don't get in the ring with anyone, Billy, you don't have to fight them,' he told me once when I asked him how he dealt with the constant abuse he received from all the gang bangers on his way to work each day. That was the most sense he ever made in one sentence. Ste was just working his ticket to freedom; we were of similar age and our personalities simply clashed. I had heard from a few people that he was one of the main boys back in his day. He had a fight with Driscoll, a black belt in karate and known as a hard man who worked on the doors of the State nightclub, a popular haunt for known drug dealers and gangs in the early nineties. The fight, I was told, went on for half an hour and with neither side inclined to throw in the towel: no loser, no winner, so you had to respect him for that.

I just wished he would have the humility to be honest and not be this grandiose drug lord, who wanted – needed – to be liked. It wasn't an attractive quality and it was sad to see him embarrass and humiliate himself like that.

I'm banged up in a cell with a lad whose name I won't even mention because he's a rat with his manky vest and bare feet. The Bruce Willis of rats. All I want to do is get through this prison sentence the best and easiest way I can. I don't want any problems, just to get in and out of this shithole as quick as possible. I find myself people-pleasing and being nice and polite, which some people take for a weakness, although in all honesty I just want to rip the windpipes out of them when they piss me off. I try not to act like that today while I'm in with the Bruce Willis-looking rat.

He's sitting on his chair eating his noodles, wearing his gym vest, with the TV remote constantly on his lap. I'm suffering dull soaps every evening, putting up with his shit and control issues, his constant texting to his girlfriend, his needy conversations and above all his stinking attitude.

Last night I got out of bed in the middle of the night for a leak; it happens a lot nowadays, the need to empty my bladder. I'm on the top bunk while the Rat sleeps on the bottom and the concrete floor is a long way down. THUD! Sixteen-stone-plus hits the ground, the knees doing their best not to buckle. The journey back up is a mission – I'm not as young as I used to be. 'What the fuck lad? Every night you do this landing with a noise by my bed,' Bruce said, his tone an ugly mix of whining and aggression, full of the injustices of his miserable life.

'Try being banged up with eighty Thais and navigating your way through a sea of bodies, most of whom were in for multiple murders, rape and would stab you in an instant if you complained about one of them getting up to go to the toilet,' I reasoned back to him. Despite that, he continued to moan. As I struggled back into bed I mumbled, 'OK, OK, no harm meant,' sounding calm but inside I was fuming. *Who the fuck is he talking to like that?* I thought to myself. *Is he taking me for a knob-head?* The resentment was building while my pride and ego felt attacked. I wanted to retaliate. The conflict I had going on in my mind was building and was dangerous. *Just let it go, Billy,* I said to myself.

'Why don't you climb out the end of the bed, instead of making a fucking noise, jumping up and down next to my head?' he rattled on, forgetting how patient and tolerant I had been. I had put up with his controlling and selfish behaviour, the territorial 'my pad' attitude, the late nights, the TV blabbing at all hours, the getting up and being mindful when the door opens so he can continue to sleep in his pit. The list is endless and the more I think about it, the angrier I became. I was really struggling not to react. It was 1.30 a.m., so I did my best.

'OK, ask me nicely and maybe I will,' I said.

I slept with resentment and awoke with a powerful need to say something to him and the need to assert myself. Conflict was imminent and I was scared of how I might react. It all had me feeling very uncomfortable indeed. The door opened for showers, phone calls and morning duties. I closed the door and looked at the Rat asleep in the lower bunk.

'Hey, lad, you need to get out of bed. We need to talk right now,' I said, my temper and voice rising an octave. Fists clenched tight, ready for action, I just wanted to dismantle his head with my bare hands.

He awoke startled and confused. 'What, lad, what's going on?' he said, suddenly realising I meant business.

'You know what's going on. I'm fed up of your shit so let's deal with it now.'

He quickly jumped out of bed, fear in his eyes. I could see he was shitting himself as he started to try and talk his way out of it, rattling on about all the time he's been away he's never had any problems or conflict until he met me. Of course, what he wasn't admitting was that he'd never come across anyone who had stood up to him and told him straight. As I squared up to him, I watched him wilt in the face of my aggression. His voice wavered, betraying his real fear.

I began to calm down, the red mists of rage slowly clearing. Only a week or so to go until he's out, I told myself. Hang in there and I'll be the owner of the TV remote, the big chair and, more importantly, the bottom bunk! I let it drop and grabbing my towel left him to sweat it out as I went to shower.

This evening, after five o'clock bang up, the atmosphere between us is tense as I watch the Rat slurping his noodles and think about ripping out his heart, but I control myself and no more is said.

A few days later, to my amusement, the security team searched all the cells on the wing looking for drugs, mobile phones and weapons. They used the wand for an all-body scan and it beeped sharply in the area of the Rat's backside. While watching this, I recalled the moment when a young Thai, who had been sent to Chiang Mai prison the same day as me, was stood in front of me in a line waiting to be routinely searched. It was early evening and eerily quiet in the courtyard when suddenly a phone rang. I watched the young Thai's face as he looked around in sheer panic. A guard came rushing over to me and I simply shrugged my shoulders. The guard then turned his attention to the young Thai, who was barely out of his teens, directing a knowing look at his backside.

'Me torasap mi?' ('You have phone?') the guard barked at the young man, who looked down and nodded.

He had secreted a phone the size of a 1990s Nokia inside the cheeks of his arse but had forgotten to switch it off. The silence of the courtyard was now torn asunder by his pitiful screams as he was ferociously beaten to a pulp in front of us.

In a full strip search, they found a phone up the Rat's arse. My phone! It was almost worth the loss to see him sweat for a couple of days worrying if the nicking he got for that would delay his release.

It didn't! I went off to the Welcome Centre one morning and when I came back, he was gone.

I hoped they wouldn't put anyone in my cell for a few days at least, but with the ever-growing prison population, I knew that was highly unlikely.

The next occupant to be in my cell companion was a young guy called Tommy Joyce – a traveller and first-time offender in for fraud. He had received a nine-month sentence for ripping off the elderly on roofing jobs. He feared getting beaten up when his crime had been written up in the local newspaper and his mugshot along with those of three of his co-defendants were featured on the centre pages.

Ste the E was on his homemade punchbag and the sound of the loud thuds resonated through the walls as Tommy entered the cell. He shuddered every time he heard the loud thwacks, looking frightened and staying silent. To be honest, I wasn't interested in small talk so was quite happy with the silence. I sat in the big comfy chair with the remote control, saying nothing, which I could see further intimidated and agitated Tommy. He introduced himself sheepishly to me after about half an hour of non-verbal communication. I didn't even respond, just grunted an acknowledgement. I was pissed off with the number of different people I had to occupy a small, hot, stinking cell with.

'Make sure he's OK, lid. He needs a bit of guidance and I thought it would be a good idea to put him in with you,' Miss D said when we got opened up after lunch. 'He seems like a good kid, just a bit misled, and he's clean, so you've got a touch there,' she added.

I just wanted to mind my own business and get on with my time. Not babysit newcomers. However, my heart wasn't that dark to the point where I'd ignore someone who was struggling to adapt to their surroundings, so I promised Miss D I would show him the ropes.

Tommy started to loosen up when I offered him a cup of coffee. We spoke at length after that about his family, his offence, the reason for it and the crowd he'd got himself mixed up with. He wasn't a bad lad. He was upset that he had to leave his girlfriend and their recently born child on the outside, and was deeply worried about his personal safety, especially in the light of the regular, harsh television news reports about this particular establishment. He'd be out in four months on his tag (home detention curfew: 7 a.m. until 7 p.m.), if only he could keep his head down.

'Here he is, the big hitter, big Tommy the tabby basher,' Ste said, taunting Tommy over his offence.

'Don't be taking me for an eejit. You don't know the full story, so be minding your own business, or me and you will be having problems,' Tommy said, getting right up in Ste's face one morning. Ste was taken by surprise and deflected it with a bit of banter. He was backing down and never said another word to Tommy after that. Although he was a first-time offender, Tommy wasn't soft and, after a few weeks away, he grew in confidence, but he was also a very sensitive family man and just wanted to go home like the rest of us, without any problems.

The day finally came for his release and, although I was happy for him, I was also sad to see him go. Miss D was right, he was a decent kid after all, and I was confident after our talks that he wouldn't be going to prison again anytime soon.

Chapter 21

Badinage

There was speech in their dumbness, language in their very gesture.

The Winter's Tale Act 5, Scene 2,
William Shakespeare

THE Mamba challenge is popular among inmates desperate for a few pipes of spice. The cannabinoid-like drug is linked to serious health issues ranging from difficulties in breathing to psychotic episodes. Yet these drugs are still in demand in prisons with inmates at risk of serious mental health issues from their habitual use.

I watch as a young lad degrades himself: running across the suicide-prevention netting naked with a toilet brush up his arse, while the drug dealers, who peddle their perpetual misery, are in fits of laughter.

Actively humiliating the vulnerable is common practice in prisons. Inmates are thrown into the big industrial tumble dryers, made to fight with each other and even sexually assaulted while under the influence of the zombie-state-inducing drug. It makes me sick witnessing this madness going on around me endlessly.

All I can do is offer those that are in the grip of this drug and others a possible way out. I share my personal journey in the recovery and twelve-step meetings, which disgracefully, considering the unarguable and highly visible drug epidemic, the prison won't provide itself. I request access to a room to set up a mutual aid group where I can tell my story and offer support. Naturally, I keep coming up against bored excuses and a couldn't-care-less attitude on the part of the authorities.

Today has been very challenging and emotional for me. I'd been feeling really fed up, losing the will to live. Trying to be there for others as well as myself has proved difficult. Oliva had laid into me on the phone, again, causing me to break down. My arrest, conviction and imprisonment has stoked her resentment and she is loaded with bitterness. I can feel how the relationship is definitely coming to an end. Trying to deal with that as well as being in prison is starting to overwhelm me. All I can do is try to keep it together and just fake it until I make it (out). Olivia hasn't written or visited for almost three months. I wouldn't mind but I've only been in prison for four months.

I picked up the phone to call her feeling unutterably sad. It had been a few hours since we had last spoken, so I was hopeful she might have calmed down by now. I selfishly knew it was all about changing the way I felt at that moment and hoped she'd understand that I was struggling. That I too needed some TLC. She answered immediately.

'Hiya, Liv, you OK?' I asked nervously.

'No, I'm not,' she replied quietly, in a childlike, whiney voice.

'I just thought I'd give you a call. See how you were feeling,' I said in my most convincing concerned voice, knowing as soon as she had answered that it was going to end up in an argument, caused by hers truly.

'I don't know why you're calling me. You know I'm not well and it's all your fault. I have NO ONE! No one at all to take care of me when I'm sick,' she said angrily before I heard sobbing.

I tried to soothe her, muttering 'Yeah, I know' and 'I'm sorry you feel this way', but all the while thinking there was absolutely nothing I could do to physically be there other than escape. She had serious health anxiety and needed a therapist to deal with her issues.

The next fifteen minutes were spent getting a list of problems and an avalanche of feelings, blame, hatred, name calling, and by the end of the phone call I wanted to end my life. It grieved me but I knew I had to accept that our relationship was doomed and remain focused on my own state of mind. I didn't want to get into a tit-for-tat argument: it was over. The way she was behaving towards me was unreasonable. I felt it was her manipulative way of breaking up with me to end our affair.

An old acquaintance of mine, Jason, was on H wing where he had been diagnosed with cancer – non-Hodgkin's lymphoma. Mark, one of the H-wing recovery mentors, told me Jason was putting on a brave face but thought it would do him the world of good if I could somehow get over to have a chat with him. I spoke with the senior officer on my wing, a harsh-looking woman who I felt uncomfortable around. She surprised me when she offered to personally escort me over to see Jason.

Later that day, I sat with Jason in his cell and did my best to reassure him that if he remained positive no matter what, he'd be OK. It felt rewarding to offer my experience and I'm sure he felt much better sharing with someone who had been down the same road. I knew that talking to someone whose situation was a lot worse than mine would also put my own problems into perspective. My life at the time wasn't that bad, and I was grateful I wasn't in Jason's headspace at that moment. I thanked the officer on the way back and noticed that underneath her reserved, even haughty, demeanour there was a lovely, kind woman. I imagine years of dealing with hardened criminals had built her a pretty tough exterior.

As the weeks went by and the momentum continued towards the release of *A Prayer Before Dawn*, I began to prepare myself for the many media interviews I'd been told to expect by the producers in Liverpool. It was difficult being in prison, especially when *I'm a Celebrity . . . Get Me Out of Here!* was on TV. The banter was relentless.

'Here is . . . the big hitter. I'm a celebrity get me out of here,' would bellow Ste the E on numerous occasions. He'd read reports published in the national papers about my escapades in Thailand. It was all harmless banter and I was beginning to warm to Ste. Turned out he could take a joke as well as give one.

'No worries, lad, I'll buy you a pair of trainers with my earnings when I'm out, ya scruff,' I laughed, throwing little hand grenades about his hidden millions. The truth was that being banged up in prison filled me deeply with shame, but I was slowly coming to terms with the acceptance and understanding I received from others.

Hamish from Altitude Films has been a good friend and we had stayed in regular contact ever since we'd met in a café in London to talk about the distribution of *A Prayer Before Dawn*. He wrote to me about a PR initiative for the film and asked if I would consent to being interviewed by Professor Green, a really well-known rap artist who was also becoming known for his cutting-edge social documentary films. The interview would be about the real 'Billy Moore' and would be shown to the *Prayer* film audience after the credits had rolled. It was about giving the people who watched my story an insight into my life today.

I was fine with it, but the prison governor would have to give her permission. It was in her gift as to whether the interview would or would not be filmed within the prison. Hamish also had Channel 4 News, the *Liverpool Echo* and the *Independent* lined up to meet me. As it turned out, the governor was fine with the interviews going ahead; it was positive PR for the prison. A change from the continual negative publicity calling out the 'inhumane conditions' uncovered at Walton. Lisa, my offender manager, arranged everything and set things up in the family visits hall.

I wasn't sure what I was going to be asked but hoped the focus would be on the up-and-coming release of the movie and not on my crime. My stance on the latter was straightforward: I broke the law and must accept the consequences. My hopes and intentions now were all geared towards helping, supporting and guiding younger members of society who were at risk of going down the one-way path of criminality. To try to articulate in our common language (as one who had been there and got the T-shirt) that there is more to life than committing crime and wasting years and years banged up in hell holes here or anywhere else.

Emily, a pretty girl in her mid-twenties and employed by Altitude Films, met me in the family visits hall. Feeling both nervous and excited, I looked around but couldn't see Professor Green. I had hoped he'd be there so we could chat a little and get comfortable before the interview, but Emily told me he was going to walk in, sit down and crack on with the questions while trying to make it as natural as possible. This was going to be awkward. I had been imagining the interview in advance, orchestrating in my head how it should play out, and now I was feeling deeply uncomfortable, properly out of my depth.

Ten minutes passed in relative silence when in walked the professor. He sat down, said hello and how much he enjoyed the movie and that was that. We had a terrific chat and I found him to be an amazing guy. He had the ability to put me completely at ease and we spoke for quite some time before he had to make way for the Channel 4 interviewer.

She seemed to approach the interview with her mind made up as she let rip about my offence and showed no interest in my story or the scourge of drugs in society and prisons. The focus was all about portraying me as a violent criminal who lacked remorse and would constantly contradict myself. Her interview was nothing more than a public flogging session and had little regard for context or important social issues. At the end of the interview I went back to my cell thoroughly dejected. I felt I had been set up.

I was relieved and grateful to read the following day the *Liverpool Echo* and the *Independent* pieces, which were more balanced and fairer than I expected. They'd clearly listened to what I had to say about the film and how prisons here in the UK had become massive mental health institutions.

HMP Liverpool holds almost nine hundred inmates. That is a huge reduction since I was last there in 2003 when it held over sixteen hundred and the overcrowding was nothing short of a national disgrace. Most inmates who were addicted back then used heroin or smoked Moroccan black cannabis resin. None of the psychotic highs that flood the prison system today were used back then. As awareness and recognition of mental health issues have dramatically increased, our medical authorities and politicians fall over themselves to recognise and embrace the problems and be seen to be 'doing the right thing'. Of course, prisoners are past masters at exploiting and manipulating even the smallest chink of weakness in the system. Prison staff, on the other hand, are equally adept at weeding out the blaggers, looking for pills or getting hold of smoking-cessation patches, which the prisoners slice up and roll into homemade cigarettes . . . Not for nothing was the Liverpool prison doctor known as 'Doctor No-meds'. While there are plenty of inmates who exploit the system, there are many more genuine sad cases of mental health sufferers in daily anguish.

I was in the healthcare waiting room one morning and it was so full you couldn't sit down. It held the usual suspects, mostly addicts looking for their next fix – anything they could scrounge off the doctor – to escape the perpetual grind of their environment. Hours spent waiting to be seen, so to pass time the younger, stronger inmates would take the piss out of anyone they thought was vulnerable. For their boredom-alleviating amusement, a young Chinese man by the name of Jack was today's choice of target. Obviously that couldn't have been his real name as he didn't speak a word of English. He had long, bleached blond, straggly hair and a goatee beard, and looked unusually skinny, almost anorexic. He stood alone in the corner with his back to the wall, clearly unnerved; the proverbial rabbit caught in the headlights. *Pure victim material*, I thought.

I observed his behaviour, which was quite odd. He was wearing his grey, prison-issue tracksuit tucked into dark grey socks with a blue T-shirt, and I noticed lumps and bumps in the lower half of his clothes. It looked like he was concealing something.

I discovered that owing to his poor mental health, he'd become seriously paranoid and was carrying all his prison belongings with him, stuffed down his trackie bottoms: plates, bowls, plastic cutlery, toiletries, even a toilet roll. He couldn't speak English and the young group of lads found it all routinely amusing to insult and abuse him. I witnessed the fear in his sad eyes and the underlying panic in his demeanour. He was scared and frozen to the spot, while endlessly enduring verbal abuse, being spat at, poked and prodded.

It took me straight back to my time in Thailand – struggling with the language barrier, not knowing what was being said to me made me paranoid. I knew how he must be feeling – only he wasn't me, because I would not have taken any shit, regardless of a potential beating.

Being a rebel without a cause, I decided to say something in his defence. 'Hey, give him break. He's obviously not the full shilling,' I

191

said, standing up and looking down at the three young 'acting tough' guys. Bullies – that's what I saw. Not one of them said anything in response to me, they just skulked away. I'm a big lad with a face that's been through the wars, so I didn't really need to say much.

But I hadn't quite finished with them. I asked them how would they feel if they were in a foreign prison alone and were subjected to the same level of abuse? They had the decency to look embarrassed, sat with their heads hung in shame – with nothing to say, finally. I was a challenge they hadn't expected and, after sharing a little of my experiences, they began to empathise and find some compassion for Jack. He smiled at me as he walked out, then about-turned and saluted, saying, 'Shee shee nee.' 'Thank you,' he'd said in his own language.

I never really knew much about mental health when I was banged up in Thailand; I just thought people were crazy and that's how it always was for them. Then I encountered poor Gogg, a Thai in his early thirties who had spent eight years on remand by the time I had arrived in Chiang Mai Central Prison. He stood out from the rest of the inmates because of the blue boxing headguard he always wore. The story was that he'd been arrested for killing his parents. I'm not sure if it was true but at some point earlier he had taken a devastating beating for his crimes and suffered permanent brain damage as a consequence.

I felt a profound pity for Gogg as he sat slobbering in his own excrement with tattoos of penises all over his body and a pair of testicles tattooed in blue across his forehead; he was a pathetic mess. I attempted to talk with him, but it was pointless. However, any small act of kindness directed towards him would prompt a beaming smile and his large brown eyes would gently light up. I would sit next to him, feeding him spoonfuls of rice and making sure he took small gulps of water. For reasons I couldn't properly explain, I felt concerned about his wellbeing. He was the most vulnerable and weak among us, entirely friendless and without support.

There were a few ladyboys who also took pity, and would sometimes leave bits food next to him. I spoke to the boxing *ajarn*, the coach I had befriended, about Gogg. He told me in his best English that Gogg was too diseased in the mind to stand trial and would probably die in prison.

Owing to the massive amounts of medication he was force fed, Gogg could hardly walk and would often fall, causing his body to be pockmarked with scrapes and open, suppurating wounds. The head guard provided him with some protection against serious injury, but in all fairness his brain was already mush and his face looked like a box of oranges with lumps and bumps everywhere.

I spent a year in Chiang Mai before I was moved to Klong Prem in Bangkok, and spent at least an hour a day just sitting in silence with Gogg. To this day I don't know what became of him and often wonder about his fate. Everything about my time spent in Thailand still haunts me – especially while I was sitting in the healthcare department of HMP Liverpool.

It was a shame to see so many young lads as well as old timers have their lives devastated by these new synthetic drugs flooding our community. The desperate levels of behaviour people resorted to in order to get high, and escape whatever torments inflicted them, was insane.

One twenty-one-year-old was instructed to run headfirst into a wall for a hit of spice, which he did without hesitation. There was a sickening thud as his head bounced off the concrete wall, blood spilling from a huge gash on his forehead. It was hard to witness and not intervene but, in a way, I was just glad it wasn't me in his position. Some people must reach their own rock bottom before making a change in their life. It's only when we've experienced enough pain that we either make a change and stop what we're doing, or we simply lie down and die. I'm only one man and would probably come dangerously unstuck if I continued to intervene in other people's battles. They needed to fight their own. I wasn't playing the hero any more. I had enough on my own plate to worry about.

I didn't look forward to my visits to healthcare, sitting in a crowded room with bullies, drug pushers and the insane. I'm certainly not out to harm or hurt anyone. I was just a guy who had lost his way in life and needed to find his own way back. The trouble was, the path I was travelling on was a minefield of inadequate mental healthcare and hair-trigger dangerous situations.

It was the sound of dogs barking that woke me from a deep sleep. I jumped out of bed and stood on the pipes to look out of the meshed window and see what all the fuss was about. It was the Northwest Tornado Team coming through the big prison gates. Was it that time of the month yet again? When the whole prison got put on lockdown and there was no movement at all throughout the day. The Tornado Team is a unit of elite officers sent into prisons to bring riots under control. They are usually made up of fifty officers who dress in Robocop-style black boiler suits and this firm means business. Hardened criminals were already panicking about losing their booty, including phones, drugs and tobacco.

Bang . . . bang . . . bang on my wall and then a voice echoed along the pipes. 'Wake up, Bill. The big hitters are here. Hide your swag and make sure your iPhone is plugged.' This was followed by a loud cackle from Ste the E. It was early, about 6.30 a.m., and the barking became louder as the elite of the prison service marched on to A wing.

'Make sure you swallow your toaster,' I shouted back.

'Del Boy . . . how are you going to survive the bang up? Get on the buzzer if you feel suicidal,' Robbo shouted from his cell on the opposite side of the landing.

The wing was alive with inmates shouting, 'Burglars are coming!', the warning shout to anyone with unauthorised articles in their possession.

I was much older and wiser these days and I had been there many years ago with all the dramas, especially when I was in Stafford prison, a Category C establishment that was the worst shithole I was ever thrown in while serving time in the UK.

You could throw lines over the outside wall from your cell and have parcels full of drugs tied onto them if you had the connections, and some inmates would ask me to throw a line over at least three times a week. I remember being on E wing – the 'basic wing' where no one got any privileges – so with nothing to lose apart from your sanity after being locked up literally twenty-three hours a day, we'd break the rules to break up the day. The prison was built in the city and you would often get young girls outside shouting up to the inmates.

'Hey, scouse, how are you doing? Are you there?' came a shout one evening from a girl standing on the opposite side of the road with a couple of her friends.

Was I here? Where else was I going to be? I thought. I was sharing a cell with a guy from Newcastle called Paul Donaldson who had a thick Geordie accent.

'Yeah, what's up, girl?' I shouted back down to her. It was late, about 10 p.m., and I could see only her silhouette in the shadows.

'Ooh-er, I love your accent. Will you say something to me?' she giggled.

'Howay man, has the lass got any fucking drugs? If she's got no drugs, ask her to send me her knickers ower on a line,' Paul said laughing. But he was also serious.

'What do you want me to say? And have you got any drugs?'

'Sorry, scouse, I've no drugs but can you say something in scouse, please?' she pleaded.

'How about chicken wings, girl?' I shouted, knowing that usually got a laugh from the out-of-towners. They always giggled at the way I said 'chikkin'.

'Nah drugs. Get her fuckin' knickers on the line then, man,' Paul interjected.

'Can you send us your knickers up, girl? It gets a bit lonely in here,' I said laughing.

'Ooh-er! I can't do that. You can have my bra if you want,' she offered.

'Howay man, it's better than nothing. Get the bra. It'll be a laugh.' Paul would be happy with any lingerie.

The line went over the wall, weighted with two thick plastic knives, the girl tied her bra on it and told us to pull it up. When it was six inches from the top, we yanked it over the barbed wire and into our cell. It was a big bra and we giggled like two schoolchildren as Paul tried it on and flaunted it around the pad under his grey prison sweatshirt.

'I look like fuckin' Melinda Messenger, man. Howay, light up a tab, man. I'm suffocating for a smoke,' Paul said as he walked across the cell like he was on a catwalk.

Suddenly the door of our cell flew open and the Burglars bounced in, surprising us. They must have heard me shouting out of the window. They saw the green line made from blanket on the bed and knew we had been up to no good. It was enough suspicion to search the cell and us.

'Hands behind your back, both of you,' demanded Mr Mason, who was a young, stocky screw who fancied himself in a fight and would throw his weight about regularly. Mr Mason, aka the 'Pit Bull' as he called himself, was accompanied by two other officers on night duty.

Paul had his arms folded across his chest to hide the two bumps protruding suspiciously from under his top.

'Moore, you first. Out here.' Mr Mason said, directing me to the dimly lit landing were a towel had been placed on the floor ready for a strip search.

'OK, you know the drill, Moore. Top first.' The drill was you removed one item of clothing at a time, usually going from top to bottom, and then a quick squat, hence the towel on the landing.

I giggled uncontrollably throughout the search, knowing how uncomfortable Paul must be feeling. The horror in his eyes as they darted to and fro, looking for any sort of escape while he hugged his chest tightly, was a sight to behold.

'Ya divvent search me, man,' he spat aggressively as Mr Mason and his two companions approached.

'We can do this the easy way or the hard way, it's up to you, Donaldson,' Mr Mason said calmly while the two taller officers stood either side of Paul, ready to take him down if he maintained his refusal. Paul walked hesitantly out of the cell and looked down at the towel sheepishly, ready to be humiliated. I couldn't stop sniggering, just glad it wasn't me.

Paul slowly took off his top to reveal the bra around his chest, his face glowing red with embarrassment.

'What the fuck are you wearing there, Donaldson?' Mason asked, pointing at Paul's chest with disbelief written across his face.

Paul looked him straight in the eyes and without hesitation said, 'It's my gym vest, boss. It shrunk in the wesh, man, that's why it's so small.' The other two officers (and I) could no longer contain our laughter. Mason didn't look impressed.

'It's a fucking lady's brassiere. What are you? A cross-dresser, Donaldson? You enjoy wearing women's underwear, do you?' Mason shouted loud enough so as the rest of the wing could hear. 'You're nicked, son, and you'll be on a governor's report in the morning for having an unauthorised article on your person – namely a woman's bra.'

The door slammed shut. We didn't say a word to each other, but the realisation of what had just occurred hit us and we burst into renewed fits of laughter.

Paul went in front of the governor the next day and got lucky with just twenty-eight days' loss of canteen. But he also got plenty of abuse from the lads, who started calling him Paula. Shouts of 'Show us your tits' became the norm, but he took the banter well.

The Burglars left just before the evening meal and at least half a dozen inmates on our wing had been caught with a wide variety of contraband: spice, phones, shivs, tobacco, cannabis . . . the list went on. The Filipino guy opposite us, who was known for his violent knife attacks, had been found with a brush pole sharpened to a point so it resembled a javelin.

'Check out Rambo over there. They found a fucking spear under his bed,' Ste said, as we were opened for our evening meal. 'See they never found your blower, hey Bill? They need to be up early to catch you, hey?'

I knew he was just checking in. Even if I had one, he'd be the last person to know. The phone I brought in with me was long gone. It was a relief – the constant plugging it in and out of my arse was painful and it was just a big headache to worry about. We have literally hundreds of things in our lives to be grateful for, and not having a phone routinely inserted into one's back passage is one of them. Days like this broke up the monotony of prison life and gave everyone something to talk about.

Chapter 22

Moods

Being once chaf'd, he cannot
Be rein'd again to temperance; then he speaks
What's in his heart.

Coriolanus Act 4, Scene 2,
William Shakespeare

Despite the drugs and insanity of Walton prison, I had managed to settle into some sort of routine. So, with the muddled logic of the British prison system, I was awoken early one morning by my cell door slamming open, light flooding the cell and a grizzled old-timer screw barking at me to pack my possessions. I was being moved. No one could or would tell me where.

Half an hour later I was standing at the transfer and discharge desk – all my possessions in the world, a few photos, some bits and pieces of stationery, tins of tuna and cheap prison-issue clothes stuffed into a sealed plastic bag. Prison admin is notorious for its clunking and hopelessly inefficient paperwork. Except, that is, when it comes to processing prisoners for transfer and discharge; in that it excels. Less than ten minutes went by and I was bundled into the back of an armoured prison bus – the feared 'sweat box'. Each prisoner is locked into a two foot by three foot cubicle that consists of a moulded plastic chair fixed to the floor, with a nine inch square window of escape-proof perspex, nearly opaque with scratches on the outside. Despite rigorous searches, over the years prisoners have managed to smuggle felt pens or sharpened plastic cutlery on board and the hard plastic interior of every locked cubicle is scrawled with the graffiti of the defiant and desperate. The claustrophobic space always smells strongly of piss.

As the bus lurched along, its noisy, gasping, diesel engine straining under the extra weight of the escape-proof armour, I slid about on the shiny grey plastic seat. No seatbelt to strap myself in – the prison service had them removed years ago and managed to gain exemption from seatbelt laws on the grounds that they were all too often used by suicidal prisoners to strangle themselves. Pulling up in a queue of traffic, presumably waiting at a red light, I was startled by a face pressing up against my grubby window – its features grotesquely distorted. There was banging on the sides of the van and jeering abuse. Despite the early hour, a gang of local lads on bikes had surrounded the van and were enjoying our plight for their own entertainment. As the bus pulled away and the traffic thinned out, an acrid smell made me draw breath. A yellow, urine-smelling puddle pooling on my floor made me jerk my feet up. My fellow prisoner in the locked box in front of me had wet himself through humiliation and fear. Soon a guard shouted at me to lift my feet higher and a filthy-looking mop appeared under the door gap.

Despite the smell, this was better than the last time I was moved from one prison to another.

My transfer from Chiang Mai to Klong Prem Central Prison in Thailand was conducted in the most inhumane way imaginable.

We were loaded into a caged van that held sixty inmates crammed up against one other in a space that half that number would struggle to fit in. The journey to Bangkok was utterly horrendous. The scorching heat was sheer torture and many inmates' faces were squashed against the caged mesh where they spent the entire journey in agony. The metal shackles around our ankles weighed three kilos and bit deep into our skin, causing endless discomfort, while all the time mosquitoes feasted on a buffet of our blood. The journey wasn't short either. I was told it would take at least twelve hours to arrive at our destination.

The two armed guards were seated in a separate cage, their hands wrapped tightly around shotguns, never taking their eyes off us as the sweat dripped down their expressionless faces.

I had managed to get one of the few seats available on a makeshift plank of wood that was fixed horizontally across the bus – reserved for the old and sick. Before my arrest, I had been run over by two cars and had recently undergone surgery. My physical condition was still poor and I feared the worst as I sat there in a hospital gown with a tube protruding from my stomach, draining excess fluid into a glass bottle. I was in severe pain and there were moments during the journey when I would have almost welcomed death as a blessed release.

After three hours had passed, I needed a toilet break. Obviously, they weren't going to pull up outside a public toilet with sixty shackled inmates. I was handed a five-litre bottle to piss in and a clear bag just in case I needed a number two. After I finished relieving myself, the bottle found its way around the rest of the bus and soon the bottle overflowed with urine, and the air was also permeated by the gag-making smell of shit. The combination of piss, shit and the incredible heat was nauseating; one inmate hurled his guts all over the metal floor adding to the noisome atmosphere.

The guards handed us each a hard-boiled egg, a fist-size ball of sticky rice and a lump of sticky brown sugar to keep us going. Water was also dished out to keep us from dehydrating. They didn't want the inconvenience of any of us dying on the way.

The journey to another establishment in the UK was going to be a walk in the park in comparison.

As the bus laboured through the Liverpool rush-hour traffic, I managed to catch sight of some road signs and the odd landmark. We were heading east out of the city. I passed the time trying to guess my destination and what route the driver would take. The first stop came an hour later when we arrived at the gates of HMP Risley, north of Warrington. My incontinent neighbour was escorted off. I soon figured out that I was being moved elsewhere as the driver set about a lengthy three-point turn and our journey continued. I had caught a glimpse of Risley's twenty-foot-high walls topped with enormous, smooth concrete tubes, designed to make climbing over them virtually impossible. Presumably they were styled to look less of an eyesore to the neighbours than the standard prison architecture of coils of razor-sharp barbed wire.

Half an hour more of the depressing journey and we pulled up at the gates of another prison. More high concrete walls and the absence of razor wire, at least on the public-facing areas. The prison service must have blown its budget – either that or the manufacturers of razor wire had run out of stock a couple of decades ago and sent all they could supply to North Korea or some other godforsaken shithole. I had arrived at my destination: Her Majesty's Prison Hindley, near Wigan to the north of Manchester.

As I was escorted off the bus, my pathetic bag of possessions pushed at me as I gingerly stepped down, old memories resurfaced. I stood in the prison yard, blinking in the summer morning sun. I had been here as a seventeen-year-old tearaway – a 'young offender'. Hindley prison had been a horrendously grim place then and hadn't improved much in the intervening years. Well, some of the buildings had new roofs, probably because the old ones were so decrepit they'd fallen in.

After my check-in process – each item rummaged through; rolled-up socks and underpants, toothpaste and toiletries carefully checked for smuggled contraband – I was allocated a cell on A-wing second-floor landing (the twos) right next door to the very first prison cell I had ever slept in. My reminiscences of my previous HMP Hindley stay were starting to engulf me. The horrible withdrawals I'd had to work through, the shits, the shivers, the sleepless nights, the constant thoughts of suicide – anything to escape the long nights I had to endure doing my cold turkey. I even remember looking out the window on one of those endless nights swearing, 'This is it. I will never come back to prison. I'll stop using . . .' but here I was twenty-eight years later, banged up in the cell next door. How the fuck had I got myself back here?

Things got better and, after a couple of days, I was offered a move to E wing and a role in the dependency recovery unit as a mentor. I gratefully accepted the offer to go over and the opportunity to attend Narcotics Anonymous meetings and possibly even get one started. It was less than a week before the release of the film *A Prayer before Dawn* and I was feeling lonely in my new surroundings. I had developed relationships with the staff and inmates at HMP Liverpool, but I was also relieved my stay there had finally come to an end because experience had taught me that friendships are a rare commodity in prison and a potential breeding ground for toxic relationships. I didn't want anything negative to impact on my recovery on release.

Walton prison is what is known as a dispersal prison where newly convicted criminals are dumped until space can be found in the wider prison estate. It has more than its fair share of oddball characters and I met plenty in my time there. I particularly liked Mac. He looked like Parker from *Thunderbirds* and was autistic, in his mid-fifties with greasy, combed-back, jet-black hair and olive skin. In contrast to his Scottish name there seemed to be a double portion of Italian in his genes. Mac would randomly tell you a joke then slide off on another completely unrelated subject. 'Why did the hedgehog cross the road? To see his flatmate,' he said, roaring with laughter. He would snare your attention and talk incessantly for hours, making absolutely no sense. He made me smile and you could see the odd combination of unworldliness and experienced hardship in his eyes. Although I liked Mac, sometimes I would have to look at my invisible watch and make my excuses while he attempted to make conversation, especially when I had work to do. Escape was an appointment I had to rush to before he had me in his Jedi mindlock for what seemed like an eternity.

Tomaz 'Seb the Lithuanian machine' was my final Walton cellmate. There was a quiet mystery about him. While I call him mysterious, lots of other prisoners thought he was fucking frightening with a face only a mother could love. And even she would harbour reservations.

Sitting at the opposite end of the cell, deep in thought after watching Piers Morgan insult his guests about their views on Brexit, he suddenly piped up. 'Billy, I ask you question?' he said, with a look of concern etched into his hard-looking, scarred face. His eyes bored into you and you knew he had seen things in war no one should ever see.

'Yes, of course.'

He stood up and faced me wearing his skin-tight, sky blue, Paisley-patterned pants that I could only describe as swimwear. He wore nothing but these skimpy numbers. He was of a similar age to me, and was short, but had a very muscular physique and the look of a Russian wrestler. In fact, in his native country he was a judo champion. Like many foreigners who got dumped into the British legal system, Tomaz was picking up a cocktail of prison slang and mangled English. Some prisoners born here can barely speak intelligible English. Tomaz's limited vocabulary was already peppered with scouse and Mancunian.

'Do you think we stay for breakfast or leave the breakfast?' he said, with a concerned look on his face.

I could hardly contain myself and, given his evident seriousness, desperately tried to stifle my laughter. Tomaz looked confused.

'It's Brexit, Tomaz, and I don't know much about it.'

I could empathise with how he was feeling. It had been the same for me when I was in Thailand and my fellow prisoners rattled away in Thai street slang, leaving me struggling to keep up.

I only spent a week sharing with Tomaz before I was transferred to Hindley prison; he was good company, a first-time offender, and didn't strike me as a villain. He was a family man who had got into debt to put his kids through school and had resorted to cultivating cannabis. Despite his hard looks and powerful physique, he was quite sensitive and someone, under different circumstances, I would have liked to have become friends with.

Hindley's Echo (E) wing was a relatively new building, built about fifteen to twenty years ago, and was full of addicts – mostly in active addiction, using spice, drinking illicitly brewed hooch and smoking dirty, stinking rolled-up cigarettes made from teabags and nicotine patches. The unit had little or no structure and most of the inmates had no idea of recovery. It reminded me of a big, out-of-control youth club. A large majority of its inhabitants were on methadone – supposedly to assist their recovery, although, in my opinion, it's difficult to find your (non-religious) soul when it is being dulled with substances. I feel strongly that total abstinence for me is the only real way to get off drugs and would encourage anyone addicted to methadone to detox especially while in prison. It is the only way to give yourself a fighting chance once released, I believe.

I'd been clean now for almost eleven months and the best part of my recovery had been spent in prison, so far without a support meeting. I looked around my new surroundings, observing everybody that walked past me. A few guys introduced themselves. One or two people on the unit understood the twelve-step programme – so that was a start. The staff that collected me, Mr Cocks and Mr Smooth, were touting for business, desperate for willing participants. I think they wanted to get this recovery wing up and running with someone to promote a positive atmosphere; it just needed that someone or something to ignite hope in the hearts of the hopeless. Echo wing was called the backdoor wing – the term used for the wing where prisoners who have snitched or ripped someone off are moved for their own safety. Others knew Echo as the smackhead wing. It had many labels attached to it, but now it was the recovery unit and the drug/alcohol team were pushing to promote a safer environment for people who wanted to find rehabilitation in the community upon release.

A couple of weeks have passed and this is the day that my interview with Professor Green is being aired on national TV. My feelings are all over the place: fear, anxiety, sadness, shame, guilt – the list goes on. I've been acting out and feel very intolerant. My anger is all based on fear. It's finally over with Olivia. Full stop. And I'm feeling the loss. The many losses, the many failed relationships, regularly find their way to haunt me. I've been feeling unhappy on E wing and it shows in my behaviour.

A young lad in his early twenties comes on to the unit and starts kicking off outside the cell he's just been allocated. 'Some dirty smackhead has left this cell looking like a shithole.' Hearing this properly wound me up. I sat there trying to control my anger, but I was fuming and felt myself being propelled towards the animated inmate screaming about smackheads.

'Hey! So tell me, what's the difference between YOU and a SMACKHEAD?' I heard myself shouting at the young lad. He looked terrified and recoiled at my outburst as I faced him down, demanding an answer.

'WELL?' I roared, fuming at this little rag-arse's attitude.

Eyes full of fear and gulping for air, he said, 'Er, nothing,' after a brief moment. 'I didn't mean it like that, Billy. I'm sorry, bro,' he stuttered, then hung his head in shame, realising he'd overstepped the mark.

I knew at that moment that I had overreacted; he already knew my name and I found out later my reputation for black moods had preceded me. I took a deep breath then sat down on the stairs as my conscience took hold. I wasn't in a good headspace myself and it reflected in my behaviour. I was super-sensitive about anything and everything.

'Come and sit here, let's talk,' I said to the younger guy. I felt guilty about reacting the way I had and apologised for my angry outburst. To my surprise he thanked me for challenging his behaviour and began to tell me the story of how as a kid he was constantly exposed to people calling his own father a smackhead. His dad, he told me, was a heroin addict and that's not easy for a young child to grow up witnessing. It's like watching your father slowly commit suicide in front of you. I started to understand that he was conditioned to repeat the names he'd heard others call his father to hide his own shame. How difficult that must have been. Our early years had been

209

remarkably similar; we had simply lived in different eras and used different drugs.

'Howay man, I'm no fucking muppet me like. Ya divvna know what I'm about,' Geordie screamed at the laundry guy. Geordie was a young man in his early twenties, tall with ginger hair and pasty white skin. He was a self-harmer and suffered with mental health issues. He was next door to me and I heard him shouting out of the window threatening to knife someone over spice. 'Here, man, don't take me for some dickhead because I've got mental health problems and I cut myself up. I'll fucking stab you on association if you haven't got my stuff.' The whole wing must have heard him.

'You OK, Geordie? It won't do you any favours kicking off like that,' I said.

'I know, man, but he's taking the piss.'

'Let it go, lad, and try and get your shit together,' I said, hoping he would see sense. He was a decent kid, Geordie, just messed up with the drugs and medication he was taking. So, with a grunt of acknowledgement, he remained quiet for the rest of the afternoon.

When the cell door was opened for afternoon activities, I headed off to the library and when I came back a few hours later I learned that Geordie had been taken to the hospital. He'd slashed his own throat. Geordie was one of many who self-harmed; the 'constant watch' cell was almost always occupied by desperate young offenders who were in fear of being beaten owing to their ever-increasing debts. Others seriously intended to kill themselves because they couldn't cope with prison life. These particular cells had no privacy at all as the cell door was gated for easy observation and every move you made was monitored 24/7 by officers assigned to cover twelve-hour shifts. You couldn't even take a shit in peace.

'If you can't do the time don't do the crime,' inmates taunted as they walked past the unfortunates incarcerated in these cells.

Manipulation is used as a weapon against the prison system; getting a place in the segregation unit is an easy way to avoid the bullies and as an added bonus it gets them extra vapes to smoke, extra brew packs of cheap prison coffee and teabags, plus visits from the prison chaplain armed with magazines and chocolate.

Suicide attempts are seen as a worthwhile risk for the extra attention; the problem is sometimes the 'attempt' ends in tragedy and if a prisoner dies in custody that's a load more paperwork for the prison system to deal with and gives the prison establishment bad press – something every justice minister and prison in the UK wants to avoid. So, the shameless, vulnerable and needy inmates use it as a terrific manipulation tactic to get their needs met.

But it's hard for poorly trained, too few in number and, frankly, indifferent prison staff to differentiate between the cynical attention seekers and the truly desperate.

Two, three or four prison suicides each week have become the norm. Black humour swiftly follows rumours of another hanging or slashed arteries. 'Can I have his trainers, boss?' or 'Don't be letting his ma have his porn mags. Give them here . . . ' echo along the landings and in the screws' ears even as the bodybag is loaded on to a trolley and taken away.

On one occasion, a young lad, whose real suicide bid had been thwarted in the nick of time by a vigilant prison officer, was explaining to me why he had hanged himself from the window bars with a strip of torn bedsheet.

'At least when I have gone someone will realise, maybe even feel sorry for me . . .'

A few weeks later, when he bled to death alone in his cell . . . no one gave a shit.

Chapter 23

Stitched

But 'tis strange:
And oftentimes, to win us to our harm,
The instruments of darkness tell us truths,
Win us with honest trifles, to betray's
In deepest consequence.

Macbeth Act 1, Scene 3,
William Shakespeare

A MEMBER of the prison substance-misuse team entered the library where I was busy typing away and asked whether she could speak to me. Who was I to say no? As I left the library two prison officers from my wing approached.

'Can we have a word, Billy?' one of them said.

'Yeah, what's this about?' I was suspicious. I could tell something wasn't right.

'We've been notified by security that they have intel that suspects you of dealing drugs. Spice, to be specific.' It was the female substance-misuse officer who had spoken.

I couldn't help myself and laughed aloud. This had to be a joke, right? I looked at the two screws who, looking particularly sombre, merely nodded at me and grunted it was true.

'Dealing drugs! Spice! Are you messing? What possible evidence do you have that suggests that I'm a dealer?' I said, simply, truthfully baffled by the accusation. My mind was racing now, and it dawned on me they were deadly serious.

'I don't get it. Do you actually believe this to be true?' I asked all three of them.

One of the screws told me he would like to think it wasn't. The substance-misuse worker added that another peer mentor had been sacked and he was also under suspicion. The truth was the other peer mentor was a drug dealer as well as getting high on his own supply. Of course, as is always the way in prison, he had got himself in debt owing to his using and now I felt I was being dragged into his conspiracy. You can't mind your own business without someone creating problems for you.

This was an outrage. All I wanted was to help others understand there was a life worth living if they addressed their drug problem, not to create more problems. I wanted to see the author of the evidence against me. The screws were being very vague in their replies, basically telling me they had had a message that reported I wasn't suitable for the role of a peer mentor on the recovery wing any more.

I was sacked on the spot – there and then. I left feeling absolutely furious. There was no way I was going to accept the injustice of being falsely accused. Back on the wing I sensed a change in the atmosphere. A few members of our meetings approached me and voiced their concerns. They were as confused and baffled as I was, and wanted to lodge complaints. *It's a free world*, I thought – and I could feel the group's unity along with the hand of friendship that was being extended to me. It felt amazing to have their support.

Our evening meeting went ahead as normal and more people than usual attended. We shared our daily reflections about losing loved ones and our priorities in recovery. We even had newcomers come and share their experiences. It was touching to hear the honesty, courage and humility in the meeting that night.

The next day I submitted my complaint form requesting some fairness and clarity about the allegation. I also put in an application asking to speak to the number-one governor. I wasn't about to have my integrity tarnished without a fight. I knew if I didn't stand for something, I would fall for anything. I'd rather be down the segregation unit for the rest of my sentence than be called a drug dealer.

I couldn't understand how I had ended up in this situation. The conspiracy theories started to manifest and the old disease of addiction was resurfacing in my mind – the resentment, paranoia, fear. How could I defend myself when I didn't even know what it was I had done? Was my Category D in jeopardy? Had someone out there set me up? Could it be a jealously inspired resentment towards me? I didn't know and paranoia creeped its insidious way into my mind. Just because you think they're after you, doesn't mean they aren't. I knew someone was well and truly stitching me up! As long as I knew I hadn't done anything wrong then it didn't matter, but I also knew that if I didn't tell my story someone would invent one for me. I have had to fight for myself all my life and now I had to fight for my rights. My life was all about fighting and this time I was fighting for the truth. The problem was when you'd cried wolf for the best part of your life, trying to convince others you were telling the truth wasn't going to be easy. Once a criminal always a criminal, and villains, to be fair, usually aren't honest.

I had been away almost seven months and had had my ups and downs. My girlfriend Olivia had left me – one more broken relationship to add to the pile. I had missed the general release of my movie. Channel 4 had slated me – accusing me of being self-serving and contradicting myself during their interview. Fuck them! They hadn't run the whole story, just edited what they wanted the public to see, portraying me not as a drug addict with human weaknesses but as a violent, unrepentant thug. Now, following this accusation of dealing spice, I felt like I was fighting a losing battle against conservative forces. I felt isolated in my quest for fairness. However, there had been joys and little gifts along the way. Addicts finding hope where there was once none.

The cell door flew open and two screws charged in. They were dressed in stab-proof Kevlar vests, helmets and black, combat-style uniforms. Well, they weren't fucking fans looking for an autograph that was for sure. This was the security snatch squad – all tooled up and playing at SAS troopers. The main cell lights slammed on and their turbo-charged flashlight torches blinded me as I shrank back on to the bunk. It was 10.30 p.m. and they had come to do a spin – a search for the supposed stash of drugs they suspected I had secreted either up my arse or in a hidden compartment somewhere in the cell. Despite having nothing to hide, the adrenalin was pumping and my heart hammered in my chest.

I was told to stand up, drop my underwear and squat. Every prisoner, no matter how hardened to the system, hates this particular degradation. It took me back to the inhumane way I was constantly searched in Thailand prisons. I was searched head to toe with a metal detector with special attention paid to my backside as hiding a mobile phone up there is widespread practice.

Disappointed, they told me to get some clothes on – I'd been sleeping in just a pair of undies. I was then taken from my cell to a freezing, empty shower room and told to wait while they conducted a full search of my cell. I sat on a cheap plastic chair and got my heartrate back under control. Calmed now, I knew they wouldn't find anything. For all the hassle, perversely things might work out in my favour: when absolutely nothing was found it might dispel their currents suspicions.

Waiting for them to return, I began to contemplate what had gone on in the last couple days: the accusations, being sacked from my prison job and the strong suspicion that someone had set me up. Out of nowhere the paranoia kicked in again. What if it was the screws? What if they were planting something on me right now? I couldn't shake the irrational fears and the what ifs kept intruding . . . Bang! The shower door bounced off the wall and a voice barked out of the darkness. 'We've finished.' As I walked back to the cell, I saw more black-clad search teams on the landing; the special force wannabes were doing the rounds this evening.

The search teams in Thailand were a different kettle of fish – altogether more forbidding and dangerous. One morning, around 4 a.m., I heard loud whistles and then shouts as our cell door was violently flung open. Immediately we were surrounded by at least thirty masked and armed guards wearing army fatigues. Some held cattle prods or had frothing-at-the-mouth Alsatian dogs growling menacingly or snapping ferociously at any inmate who moved. Any who did were rewarded with a sharp bolt from the cattle prod.

We were all ordered to stand up and place our hands behind our heads while the cell was ripped apart. Then we were marched in single file to the compound to be searched both externally and internally. I stood watching nervously as inmates who had the misfortune to be caught with contraband were kicked repeatedly in the head and body by the guards' black-laced, steel-capped army boots. Soon both the inmates' faces and the guards' boots were covered with dark crimson blood.

The young Thai in front of me had kicked his T-shirt towards me just before I was searched. The guards found a number of ya ba tablets in the seam and assumed the top was mine. I was quickly thrown to the ground and screamed at for what seemed like forever. 'Ari farang, ya me mi.' I knew enough Thai to understand that they were convinced the drugs were mine.

'Mi me kraph, mi me ya kraph,' I screamed, protesting the drugs didn't belong to me. Prisit, the head commando, crossed the courtyard and loomed over me as I grabbed the shirt and tried to pull it on. It was far too small.

'See? It's not mine. It's too small for me. It doesn't fit,' I shouted desperately. I was terrified I was going to be sent back to the punishment cell. Now I was crying.

Prisit looked at the T-shirt and then at the guy in front of me who by now had an obviously worried look on his face. The next thing I knew the young Thai who had tried to stitch me up was being dragged away for a severe beating. Prisit looked at me again but said nothing. Some of the young Thai's friends stared at me then drew the universal cutting motion across their throats. What did they expect? That I take a beating and get thrown into punishment to protect one of theirs? I had no loyalty to any of them and only wanted to save my own arse. These were my thoughts as the screws left me alone in my cell in Hindley to clean up their mess that evening.

The next day, the whole of Hindley prison was searched, every single cell was spun. A few of the cleaners on our wing got turned over and came out shouting the odds about grasses. It was obvious to everyone that their behaviour and suspicious activity led them to being searched. A few lads were shitting themselves at being labelled a grass and were stressing to me about it. I felt the change in the atmosphere and was afraid of how I would react if someone was to provoke me.

I spoke to the governor about the injustice of what had happened to me and asked him if this allegation would affect my Cat D. He told me it wouldn't and although I felt he was being straight with me, which made me feel a bit better, I still didn't know who or what to believe any more. I had worked hard for the first time to earn the opportunity to serve the remainder of my sentence in open prison conditions, the elusive Category D. A privilege given to the lick-arses of the prison system or grasses. Only I was neither. I was just playing the game a lot more maturely as the years went by. Conforming, for the first time in my life, to prison rules and regulations.

I was too old for all this carrying on and kicking off in jail.

Chapter 24

Sabotage

Though those that are betray'd
Do feel the treason sharply, yet the traitor
Stands in worse case of woe.

Cymbeline Act 3, Scene 4,
William Shakespeare

A MORE comfortable form of prison life, influence over prison 'politics' and being part of the 'gentlemen's club' are reserved for the select few who feel they are better than everyone else because they've never used drugs such as heroin and crack cocaine. They class everyone else who has as *scum*. Or perhaps they think of themselves as merely a better class of scum. Their collective idea of having fun is to brew prison hooch, get pissed and cause as many problems as possible for other inmates: the vulnerable heroin and crack cocaine addicts who are doing their best to address their enduring drug problem.

The last thing anyone needed was a bunch of control freaks throwing their weight about, just because they wanted to continue drinking and holding their 'secret' hooch parties every evening.

To be honest, it didn't bother me what they got up to in their free time as long as they kept out of my way. I wasn't here to build deep, meaningful friendships and wanted out as quickly as possible. I hated every day of HMP Hindley; it was like a children's home – full of insecurities, immaturity and out-of-control egos.

Over the last week the atmosphere on E wing had changed for the worse. Inmates were being bullied by wing cleaners and servery workers who seemed threatened by the presence of a group of guys who only wanted to find a new and better way to live. They didn't like the idea of losing control and becoming a minority. They wanted the unit to remain their little domain and resented the changes that were becoming obvious as more and more people got involved in recovery. Paranoia permeated the unit; inmates were whispering, 'There's money on his head,' or 'He's getting it . . . ' Even my neighbour Geordie became a target. I observed a group of cleaners surrounding and backing him into a corner while making threats on his life. His eyes darted left and right and his fists were clenched tight, readying himself for an impending attack. The screws heard the commotion and slowly positioned themselves so they could intervene if things turned nasty. The group became aware of the attention they had attracted and disbanded, slithering off like so many disgruntled, underfed reptiles. Geordie banged himself up in his cell to avoid further confrontation. However, it wasn't over yet, and you could sense the looming, inevitable storm.

The next day found everyone unnaturally tense and it all began with my neighbour Max, a harmless guy who was small and physically unwell, with a face that screamed 'I've used drugs and abused myself for many, many years.' He had allegedly ripped off a guy called Nigel with a blag teabag and a nicotine patch. It hadn't been the good old posh PG Tips but a prison-issue variety coupled with only a piece of plastic from the back of the nicotine patch. Not the patch itself, you understand. You might say, so what? But this is prison life. Max received a punch from one of the older cleaners for the crime committed against Nigel, which was bang out of order as Max couldn't or wouldn't defend himself from any physical assault. Other inmates were vocal in their condemnation of the attack, calling the culprit a bully.

By this time, I was on my way to the gym. Grateful to be off the wing for an hour or two and away from all the parodies and exaggerations of prison life. On returning to the wing, I noticed Geordie sitting on the pool table and a small group of inmates talking to Max, offering sympathy. I was struggling with my hearing (I'd had my ears syringed the day before) and heard a shout coming from the upper landing from one of the arrogant young servery workers.

'Hey, Geordie! Come up here now, ya fucking gobshite, get in the laundry and let's deal with this.'

'I'm not coming up there when there's six of youse and only one of me. Do ya think I'm daft, man!?'

'Haaaaa, ya shithouse,' came the reply and a chorus of laughter from the others congregating around Geordie's tormentor.

Geordie looked up, the anger visible in his face. By now he was the focus of every inmate's attention as well a few screws who were nervously watching as things began to escalate. The next thing, Geordie jumped off the pool table and was marching up the stairs, one hand deep in his pocket. It was game on. As he neared the gang, who were still goading and threatening him, he took his hand out of his pocket, lifted it high above his head and swung it down in an obvious slashing motion. The bravado of the gang evaporated like morning mist. Cowed, they retreated from him, while down on the lower landing inmates were screaming, 'GO ON, GEORDIE LAD!'

As the gang tried to back off, a shout went up, 'He's got a blade!'

The screws came to the rescue. The weapon supposedly ended up on the floor and a young servery worker called Shirley, thanks to his habit of wearing an Alice band to restrain his long, curly hair, yelled, 'It's on the floor boss, look there,' pointing and making a kicking motion as if to push it towards the screws. Now, whether Geordie ever actually had a blade was never fully established, but that's not the point; he felt threatened, alone and in fear of his life. In my opinion a blade is not something you should be carrying around, but we were in prison and sometimes there is no other way to defend yourself and stay alive.

The screws grabbed hold of Geordie and frogmarched him down the stairs where, at the bottom, another fight erupted. All I could see were arms and legs flailing everywhere. The alarm started wailing as the whole wing erupted into violence. There was yelling and screaming all over the place. While all this was going on, I could hear my name being shouted. 'You knew about this, Billy. You're backing the wrong side.' It was the older guy who had punched Max shouting down to me. He had plenty more to say but I was struggling to hear with my bunged-up ears and everything else that was going on.

'You're backing the wrong side. You knew about this. I've got three witnesses,' I just managed to pick out from all the other noise assaulting my ears. Back in my cell I struggled to understand what had just happened and resented my name being brought into all this bullshit. Witnesses? To fucking what? This all seemed a bizarre plot to sabotage everything I had worked hard to achieve, and it was really starting to piss me off.

The rest of the bank holiday weekend rolled by without incident, but the atmosphere remained tense. Max spoke to me through the pipes and told me he wanted to end his life. Geordie had been moved off the wing for his own safety and threats were made through a window to another inmate. My name was shouted by the older guy again. I heard things such as 'Billy's little soldiers' and 'Billy giving out his orders.' I forced myself not to react because I knew to do so would place me square in the middle of the problem. These people were deluded and I had no idea why they held such a negative view of me. Maybe promoting a positive atmosphere intimidated them? Would there ever be any peace and quiet?

Why do some people resent others finding recovery? Well, my understanding is that their insecurities become a jealous obsession; their own failures dictate they must see others fail as well – to maintain equivalency and retain status. The great American writer Gore Vidal once wrote, 'Whenever a friend succeeds, a little something in me dies.' And that about sums it up.

The NA groups are a place for addicts to go and share their experiences, gather strength and hope for the future. Anyone is welcome. The only requirement for membership is a desire to stop using, and the message is simply that any addict seeking recovery need never die from this disease. It had been a struggle for the past week not to react to the provocations and to continue to practise the principles of recovery. The meetings were under threat, the atmosphere and anxiety levels members experienced were becoming problematic. Paranoia runs were going unchecked and the fear of conflict had everyone on permanent high alert with adrenalin coursing through their systems. Not healthy. This was not how it was supposed to be. The recovery staff, I felt, had not been very supportive; we struggled to find trust in the service they provided. Damaging allegations had been thrown about left, right and centre; rumour-fuelled distortions that we had meetings to discuss our drug deals were being reported; it was said I was a possible leader of a cartel who handed out orders to my little soldiers. All absolutely fucking bollocks!

I found it amusing that the only way our brave friends could relay these malicious stories to the prison staff was by way of notes in the suggestion box. The reality was the culprits actually hadn't got the balls to say any of it to my face.

I am taken out of the library by two staff from E wing for the second time in less than ten days. Unsurprisingly, with everything that has gone on and the snitching, I am worried but quickly have my concerns put to rest. I am told that the SO (senior officer) wants to speak to me in his office.

'Hello, Billy. Sit down, mate.' The SO is a youngish guy, probably in his early thirties, with a bald head and a ridiculous hedge of a hipsterish, ginger beard.

'What's all this about?' I ask, my suspicions renewed.

'I've got some bad news. We need to move you off the wing. I'm going to be straight with you. Your name keeps cropping up and you've just got your Cat D, and the truth is we don't want anything fucking it up . . .' he said, with a look of actual concern before continuing, '. . . however, it's not all bad news. I've arranged to have you put on J wing in a double cell on your own.'

J wing, the enhanced-status wing. A double-sized pad all to myself. 'OK, that's fine.'

The SO is visibly relieved by my apparent reasonableness. From what he's been told about me, I imagine he was expecting me to kick off big time.

'Er, thanks for taking it so well. We'll have you moved over before tea.'

'Off the record, what's been going on?' I ask.

'To be honest, the other mob, the cleaners, keep putting in apps about you, and when they're on apps we can't let it go under the radar, so to be fair to you, we're doing our best to keep you safe and have you out of here as soon as possible.'

I packed my bags, getting plenty of vicious, throat-slitting looks from some of the cleaners. As I walked past the older one with the blame-thrower, the one who had chinned poor Max, he gave me the Cat A stare. I looked him straight in the eyes as I walked past, staring him out.

'I'll see you on the outside,' he said, a perverse, unreasoning hatred etched into his drug-addled face.

I chuckled as I reasoned the *only* person he would be bothering to seek out on release would be his drug dealer of choice. But then I found part of me wishing that someday he'd find recovery and peace in his life.

I was sad to leave the E wing but was confident the meetings would continue and hoped to see some of our members out in the community one day.

The same evening, I received my complaint form back from security. It said they were not willing to reinstate me in my mentoring job. That they had looked into the allegations and found there was sufficient evidence to indicate my involvement in suspicious and illicit activity . . . However, they also claimed that they had no involvement in sacking me from my job. What bullshit and lies were these? I could have wasted hours trying to second-guess the reasons why the drug/alcohol team wanted shot of me, but what purpose would it have served?

The rumours became wilder as the weeks passed. Prison is a snake pit of whispers and gossip and I wanted no part of it. But inevitably some of the stories filtered down to me while I sat in the library minding my own business. 'I heard Geordie got paid half a sheet to slash the other fella,' one guy tells me. 'All the young offenders were running around doing the graft for you,' another said.

It was all bullshit and it took me back to the time when I was locked up in Chiang Mai. I had been put in punishment for three months, isolated from the rest of the prisoners, for fighting. When I came back on normal location some of the guys told me they had heard that I had been chained to a wall and beaten regularly, and that they could hear me howling in the early hours of the morning. Simply untrue, nothing but Chinese whispers.

Only we ourselves know the truth. I read somewhere that the truth defends itself – only lies need defending all of the time.

Chapter 25

Reflections

Looking on the lines
Of my boy's face, methoughts I did recoil
Twenty-three years, and saw myself unbreech'd,
In my green velvet coat, my dagger muzzled,
Lest it should bite its master, and so prove,
As ornaments oft do, too dangerous:

The Winter's Tale Act 1, Scene 2,
William Shakespeare

JWING was quiet and very relaxed. In fact, you might compare it to a care home: no chaos, no dramas, all pretty boring really with a total of just twenty-five inmates. I got speaking to a few of them – none of whom had an addiction problem or so it seemed. I talked to one young man in particular, twenty-one-year-old Leon, who told me his story.

He said that when he was fifteen years old he had almost been murdered one night after he'd been drinking heavily. He and a few friends were at a party when the mother of the girl whose party it was came home unexpectedly and sent everyone packing. On his way home, he bumped into a lad known as Teeth – his nickname derived from his big, ugly, yellow mouthful of crooked teeth. Teeth's ex-girlfriend Lottie was a friend of Leon, and Leon had heard her talk about Teeth beating her up on more than one occasion. Fuelled by alcohol and angered about Teeth's treatment of Lottie, Leon decided it was a good idea to chase him. Teeth pedalled off on his bike with Leon and his mates chasing on foot. They caught up with Teeth as he dumped his bike and ran into a house, slamming the door behind him. Leon's gang started kicking in the door but, once Leon was inside, he found himself alone. His friends had run off and left him to it. Still in a rage, Leon charged up a flight of stairs only to discover that Teeth was on home territory and backed up by eight or nine others. The tables were well and truly turned. Someone hit him from behind with a cricket bat, rendering him unconscious.

He woke up in a room alone, struggling to breathe and feeling heavily winded. He crawled on his hands and knees to the door and slowly, step-by-step with plenty of stops to rest, made his way down the flight of stairs. Reaching the bottom, he was mauled by a huge dog. Things weren't getting any better. The front door was locked and he couldn't summon up the strength to unlock it. Suddenly the door crashed open and in ran one of his friends. All he could remember saying to Gary, his friend, was that he had been hit with bats.

Gary helped Leon up and they staggered to the nearby kebab house where the rest of his friends were waiting. Leon slumped against the shop's window before slowly sliding down to the floor, leaving a visible trail of blood. Someone screamed. His coat was undone and lifted away to reveal numerous puncture wounds bleeding profusely. It was then that Leon fainted.

He recalled waking up in hospital and pleading with the doctors to tell his mother how much he loved her if he should die. The next day he found himself hooked up to all kinds of hospital machines and his abdomen hurting like buggery where he had been gutted like a fish. It turns out he was being held together by a total of fifty staples and, at one stage, had technically died on the operating table. Luckily, they had been able to resuscitate him, but it had been touch and go.

He later learned he had been stabbed a total of thirteen times: four knife wounds and nine screwdriver punctures. Three of the puncture wounds were millimetres away from his heart and one had punctured a kidney. The bat he was hit with had left him permanently deaf in his right ear.

Teeth was twenty-one and his dad was forty-eight. They, with three others, had been the ones who had stabbed him. Yet Leon never complained to the police because he held to the conviction that, one day, he would have his own revenge.

My conclusion after hearing this story was how lucky this young man was to be alive. Knife crime has become a deadly epidemic on our streets and I would like to be of benefit to our youngsters, to educate them and show them that there can be a way out. As for Leon and his thoughts of revenge, I suppose it is understandable. Of course, he could either end up dead enacting his retribution or, more likely, spend the rest of his life in prison. Where would that leave his poor mother then?

Years ago I had the misfortune to be stabbed in the chest by a local gangster, a dangerous individual who was a known knife carrier. It was the early hours and I was on my way to score drugs in the Toxteth area of Liverpool. Across the street I heard a young girl screaming. I saw a seriously big guy had hold of her elbow while slapping her repeatedly across the face. Growing up, I had already seen enough of my father hitting my mother and watching the girl getting a hiding really pushed my anger button.

I ran over, shouting at the big lump of a guy to leave her alone but when I looked into his drug-fuelled eyes I knew then and there he wasn't the full ticket. He roughly pushed the girl away and from somewhere produced a huge kitchen knife. The next thing I knew he was running full tilt at me, waving the knife in my direction. I dodged and weaved, shouting at him to fight me like a man. That was not his purpose: he didn't want to *fight* me, he wanted to *hurt* me. He couldn't get close enough to use his knife and after several indecisive minutes decided to give it up as a bad job. He and the girl (who all the time had been urging him to 'cut the bastard') flagged down a taxi. My pride wouldn't let me back down. Of course it wouldn't. It had me walking over to the taxi for one last confrontation. As he went to climb into the taxi, I pulled him out and he responded by stabbing me in the chest. I slumped to the floor and sat on my arse as the taxi drove away, the guy looking out of the rear window and grinning like a maniac. I was lucky not to have been killed. The knife had penetrated the left side of my chest on target for my heart. By sheer good fortune the guy had not pushed hard enough to cause me any serious harm. My upper body was quite muscular and I was wearing a thick hooded top – both of which counted in my favour in the final analysis. To this day I have the scar, among many, that reminds me how lucky I am to be alive.

It had been more than two weeks since I'd been re-categorised and yet here I was – still waiting. I was missing the meetings and their absence had a noticeable effect on my mood. I isolated myself on J wing where the long hours locked up had me thinking. The fear of being alone scared me; would I ever find my soulmate? I'd been thinking about my ex recently and it had left me feeling despondent.

They say when addicts are alone, they are in bad company. So true. I was confused and consumed by thoughts of love and sorrow.

Passenger's 'Let Her Go' seeped from my small radio. I tried to make sense of life from the song's lyrics and think how strong one must be to simply walk away from someone you love. This was what I had to do to save my own sanity and it was one of the most painful decisions I have ever had to make. Still, I couldn't stop thinking about reconciling with her. I was only human. By nightfall the tears were flowing down my face after a day of examining my pierced heart.

The innocent members of our family are the ones we hurt the most because we take them for granted. To win back the hearts of our loved ones, we must prove we are no longer prisoners of addiction; we must fight and not surrender to the obsessive desire that plagues our daily minds. Every form of addiction is bad, no matter whether the 'drug' is alcohol, opiates or love. I don't believe astrology has any basis in the truth, but on that day, I picked up my local paper and read:

> *CAPRICORN*
>
> *It is said the while great minds discuss ideas, small minds talk of people, so be wary of gossip. It has a habit of rebounding tenfold. While someone special is on your mind, aspects indicate you are remembering them as you wish they were, rather than the person they actually are. It is better to always trust more in your intuition.*

I read it over and over again. I could hardly believe how prescient it was. 'Trust more in your intuition.' That kept me in the present moment. It wasn't all bad. was it, Billy? It was. It really was, in fact, a living nightmare. The constant blame and control had me stressed out. I thought on balance the best thing for me would be to be on my own from now on, and not in a physical relationship. What to do on release had me worried too. No employment, no home and no money. Life can be tough, but at least I was clean and in recovery. It was now only a matter of months before I was due to be released back into society and it scared me because I had no idea what to expect. I would have to live with my mother and her partner while I was on a tag for four-and-a-half months. These were just some of the thoughts I had to deal with while locked up.

On top of this, I had not been fully able to excise my sense of injustice, and the isolation meant my initial disbelief about the ludicrous drug-dealing accusations had quietly transmuted into sleepless nights of paranoia. I honestly began to think there was a grand conspiracy to do me harm. To foil any real chance I had of redemption; of leaving prison a changed man. But things resolved themselves in the light of a new day, as they often do, when the author of the allegations cropped up in a conversation that took place while I was in the prison healthcare department. One of the younger officers explained to me how another screw – a middle-aged woman who was actively disliked by most of the prisoners and, frankly, most of her work colleagues – was the reason I had lost my job and had my reputation unfairly impugned.

Now things made sense and I could recall the day when matters had come to a head: my job required me to visit A wing, the induction unit, and this is where I went each morning to wait for the newcomers to be processed. That day I needed to use the toilet. Desperate to relieve myself, I walked upstairs to use a friendly inmate called Ryan's loo because there were no toilets for public use on any of the wings. I was stopped in my tracks by a female officer, a real jobsworth, who I knew from E wing. She stood there wearing a pair of blue rubber search gloves and waving a search wand.

'Where are you going?' she asked, eying me up and down suspiciously.

'I need to use the loo, miss.'

'Well, you can't come up here.' Her tone suggested I was up to no good; so much so, I immediately felt (and I suspect, looked) guilty.

'I'm desperate. I really need to use a toilet, miss,' I pleaded. This was like being back in primary school.

'Well, you can't come up here. Ask someone down there to let you use a toilet,' she said dismissively.

'OK, no problem. I didn't know there was a toilet down there.' Thanking her, I headed back down the stairs, thinking nothing more of it.

It was this innocent exchange that had led to the accusation of me being the number-one drug dealer in the prison. No evidence to indicate anything other than I genuinely needed to relieve myself. And all the grief that followed thereafter. My sense of injustice was profound, and I felt an unappeased anger towards the female screw. How could anyone justify sacking someone for wanting to use a toilet? What could possibly have prompted her misguided suspicions about my behaviour? I get it that people will take advantage of the roles they have conferred upon them and, in a prison, petty jealousies and envy are endemic, and a screw's job is to always be distrustful (believe the worst in humankind and they will rarely disappoint), but a blind man could have seen I was only trying to promote positive outcomes for the prison. Well, it was what it was . . . a pain in the arse, but too damn late to do anything about it.

Some further reflections on prison life.

My time behind my door usually begins at 7 p.m. I watch a few programmes, write a few letters, read a little, then get ready for bed. I awake and repeat – over and over again. Lately, I've been feeling unsettled and finding it difficult to sleep. Or I wake in the early hours, thinking of my ex-partner while waves of loss wash over me. Drowning in sadness. As the long hours of sleepless solitude pass, I have a stark mental image of standing alone in a vast wasteland of misery and solitude for all the years to come. I decide to write a letter to Olivia. I would regret not trying but doubt it will make any difference. Maybe it is my way of letting go. If anything at all, I wish her all the best for the future, she deserves it. She too has had a troubled past.

My family and friends visit regularly and tell me to keep my chin up; and that's what I do! Shit happens and I have to deal with it. But make no mistake, it means a lot to receive their love and support. Someone has just told me that the old boy who threatened me on E wing a few weeks ago has been moved to C wing for allegedly being involved in the distribution of drugs. He also claimed it was my doing that caused him to be moved and, apparently, I had put a hit on him. The rumours that fly about prison amplify and exaggerate as they travel along a pipeline of lies.

I've been told the meetings on the wing continue to flourish, something I was glad to hear. A young guy who was mad for spice has turned up, determined to stop using and give life a go. It brings a smile to my lips and joy to my heart.

Inside Time, the national prison newspaper, has published my story along with an old picture of me that the *Liverpool Echo* had published a couple of years before. The story largely regurgitates the Channel 4 report with a little bit of judicious editing and was a decent enough article.

I only hope that I will be transferred to open conditions soon so I can begin my resettlement back into society. In a way, I've felt stitched up in this prison and I sometimes wonder what kind of reaction I would have received if I was a non-compliant inmate. So, each morning I pray for the courage and strength to stay clean and in recovery for that day. Not only does it save me, but it saves everyone around me from having to deal with a living nightmare . . .

I'm told that there's a bus to Thorn Cross Category D prison this week and my hopes rise. Surely I'll be on the list to be transferred?

But I am seriously pissed off when I'm told by a member of staff on the wing there is nothing in the diary for me this week. Then I hear from another inmate that there is another bus to Thorn Cross this morning, but, again, I am not on the list – although a guy who got his Cat D *after* me is on the bus. I guess you can work out for yourself what's happening here. I've done everything they have asked of me. What more is it they want? I speak to the governor, who is as confused as I am that I am still here. He had been told I was going last week and promises to look into it urgently. I don't want to be putting in complaint forms but soon I won't have any alternative if I don't get answers.

Another inmate told me how he had been a model prisoner, behaved respectfully but lost it one afternoon, smashing his cell up and punching hell out of the walls, breaking his hands in the process. The frustration had become too much to bear. He felt he wasn't being listened to and this is what it took to get the attention he deserved. He got his answers that day. I don't want to go down such an extreme path, but I can see things heading that way.

I have just been called back to the wing. The governor wants to speak to me.

'Hello, Billy, let's get straight to it, no bullshit. I hope you don't mind Mr Rodgers being present but it's nothing other than me being as straightforward as I can here.' He paused for a moment to collect his thoughts. 'Security have tried to re-cat you because of what happened on E wing. I've stepped in and it's not happening because I don't believe any of what's gone on up there. About you and your so-called boys.'

I listened anxiously, wondering where this was heading.

'So, this is what *is* happening. I've spoken to allocations and you're now at the top of the list.'

Now I knew the reason why everything had been delayed.

So, at last, the time had come to move, and you couldn't move me quick enough. A powerful sense of relief swept through me as I left the prison on my way to my final staging post to freedom.

Chapter 26

Happy?

There is a kind of character in thy life,
That to the observer doth thy history
Fully unfold. Thyself and thy belongings
Are not thine own so proper as to waste
Thyself upon thy virtues, they on thee.

Measure for Measure Act 1, Scene 1,
William Shakespeare

THORN Cross prison was unlike any prison I had ever been in. It promoted independence, responsibility and resettlement.

Ray and Willo introduced themselves to me as prison mentors. They were both very friendly, but there was something distinctly odd about Ray. He was young, mixed race with a hint of Asian in his looks, and would ask me every five minutes if I was happy.

'Are you happy, Billy?' Ray asked, standing there rubbing his chin like a spiritual guru deep in profound thought.

'I'm happy as can be, Ray,' I replied, jovially . . .

'Good! I'm happy you're happy,' he said, then added, 'Out of ten, how happy would you say you are?'

'I'd say about an eight, Ray.'

'OK, OK. That's good. Anything above a six is good, above average,' he said while his head bobbed up and down in excited acknowledgement. Little John popped his head out of his door.

'Hey, John . . . and how are you, lad? Are you good?'

'I'm good, Ray, and before you ask, I'm about a ten,' John responded quickly.

'That's good. In fact, that's more than good. That's beautiful. Have you met Hollywood? Say hello, Bill,' he said, nodding towards me, arms folded across his chest with one hand holding his chin. He began to tell John my story.

John looked shocked. 'Fuck me, mate, how did you survive in one of those places? See me, I'd have to go up to the biggest, hardest motherfucker in there and suck his dick,' he said with a seriousness that had me and Ray doubled up in laughter.

'That's the one, John. Staying alive. I like it,' Ray said, still laughing.

All this time Willo was stood behind Ray, smiling and mimicking his demeanour: his hand on his chin, head bobbing up and down. It was good to finally be around my own kind having a bit of banter.

I found out later that Ray had a genuine germ phobia and would never let you shake his hand. He suffered with OCD (obsessive compulsive disorder) and would wash his hands constantly.

If he caught you on a bad day, he could annoy the life out of you. It took me a few weeks to come to terms with his odd behaviour, but once I got it, he was pleasant enough to be around. Ray was small in stature and threatened to tap you out if you got on his nerves, but he brought a smile to my face and he was like the unit detective: you couldn't get anything past him. Willo and Ray made me feel welcome in my new surroundings.

I was thankful to be away from Hindley. It had taken its toll on me mentally and robbed me of the opportunity to get to my meetings. The meetings in Thorn Cross took place each Thursday evening so the day after arriving I got to go to one. Over the next couple of weeks, I made the suggestion to the drug and alcohol team about setting up an internal meeting for the guys during the weekend. They thought it was a good idea and we soon had it up and running on Sunday evenings. I soon dawned on me that not many addicts made it to open prisons; they were always fucking up in closed conditions and not making it this far. Nevertheless, the message was here for them if they ever arrived.

My sister Kelly had been diagnosed with cancer and was preparing for surgery. I spoke to the chaplaincy about going home for a few hours to spend time with my family, to be there in a supporting role. I only had seven weeks before release so was classed as low risk. The arrangements were made and I was escorted from the prison for a few hours at home with my family. My mother opened the door and the first thing I did was give her a big hug. We enjoyed a meal and a few hours together before the staff member and I returned to the prison.

'How much are you getting for this movie?' somebody asked as we walked the perimeter of the prison grounds. I never had an answer to that question. Partly because I didn't actually know and largely because it was a personal matter. If, however, you asked me how I felt about the authenticity of the film, I'd give you my honest opinion. The truth was, in my naivety, I'd agreed a pretty poor deal in the contract. Show business, once the show stops, is all business – and devil take the hindmost. I'd learned my lesson. All I yearned for now was to be able to get out of prison, get back on my feet and, above all, to be happy and healthy.

A young, attractive screw called Hannah was my escort to the hospital where I was due to have my bloods tested at the Linda

McCartney Centre. As a cancer survivor, this sort of routine testing can be a deeply anxious time – but today I was feeling strong, confident and positive. An old acquaintance called Tommy happened to be in the phlebotomy clinic.

'Hello, Billy. How are you, mate? You're looking well.'

'I'm OK, Tommy. It's good to see you.'

'Fancy a coffee?' he asked.

'I'm with my escort,' I explained, pointing at Hannah. I quickly realised I had given an entirely erroneous impression and that now Tommy was smiling broadly and repeatedly giving me knowing winks.

Tommy departed, still none the wiser, and it was a pleasure to spend an hour or two sitting in a typical busy coffee shop with a young, pretty girl, drinking an Americano. For someone whose life has been so circumscribed by prison, such normality, however short in duration, is a balm. For those few hours life seemed to regain its normality. Something every prisoner craves. The prison bars had melted away like a bad dream and I felt, briefly, like a free man.

The oncologist called me into her office to tell me that my bloods had come back all OK, which was great news, but then I remembered that my sister Kelly was in the same hospital, recovering after her major surgery.

I had been training hard since I'd been at Thorn Cross, getting up early every morning to do cardiovascular workouts. My daily routine started at 6 a.m. with prayer and meditation and, by now, I had started on an intermittent fast along with a disciplined routine in the gym. All this was in preparation for the next step on my journey of being released. It was imminent and I was feeling anxious.

'How are you, Billy? Are you OK? Because you've been acting a little strange today,' Ray said. He had noticed I wasn't myself. 'Can I ask you a question? It's quite personal and I don't want you to take offence, but have you relapsed?' It was an unlikely question given our circumstances, but I suppose my behaviour had been out of sorts lately.

I looked him straight in the eye and told him that I hadn't. If I had, I wouldn't be standing here now talking to him, I thought to myself.

'Hmm, good, I'm glad to hear that. You had me worried for a couple of days,' he said, looking me up and down suspiciously as if still in doubt.

'I've just been thinking about a lot of stuff lately. The things I've lost,' I said, feeling sorry for myself and wondering why I felt the need to explain myself.

'Billy, look at what you've got. A roof over your head, food in your stomach and people who love you. OK, it's not the ideal place, prison, but you've got family out there who care. Am I right?' It was a statement more than a question.

'You're right,' I answered, knowing that my brother Joe, my mum and her partner were looking forward to me coming home on Christmas Eve.

'I'm the same, but look, we are both rich with life, we can rebuild what we've lost again, stay positive,' Ray said, catching me off guard. His wisdom-infused words hit me hard and made me realise that I was only human and that my struggles were not ones I had to deal with alone.

We don't always realise how lucky we are to be alive. Day release is a privilege inmates can earn while held in open conditions – a chance to spend a proper amount of time with your family, to build the all-important personal relationships that will be so vital as you come to terms with life outside prison. A low-risk opportunity to adjust to the outside after spending years locked up. I had only been at Thorn Cross a couple of weeks when a young guy from Liverpool, on day release, had been shot dead. The atmosphere in the prison was funereal. Actually, it turns out that I had met the guy briefly in Walton a few months earlier. He was quiet and minded his own business while on A wing. We'd spoken briefly and only in passing but he struck me as polite and respectful.

Lawrence was a Glaswegian lifer convicted of setting fire to his wife almost fifteen years ago. He worked in the prison kitchen and was coming to the end of his tariff. Lawrence would steal the odd bit of chicken to make ends meet and sell it to the lads for a packet of tobacco. I asked him one day if he could get me some chicken, just to help with my protein intake.

'Nay problem, pal. This wee shipment here is for Big Bob, so I'll get you some next week when we've another delivery.' His smile was disfigured by tobacco-stained teeth that hadn't seen a toothbrush since the day of his arrest.

Bob was over six feet tall, loud and aggressive with it. He was the number-one unit cleaner, and had taken on this mighty responsibility with relish, certain that it conferred the right to dish out orders left, right and centre. He was forever telling everyone what they needed to do and where they needed to be. Bob was clever and would pick his mark . . . using the more vulnerable, impressionable inmates to do his errands. Lawrence, he thought, was one of those inmates, and wasn't at all happy when he learned Lawrence was supplying me with the odd piece of chicken.

'Hey, Billy, don't be trying to muscle in on our graft. You know what you're doing,' Bob said one day while I was cooking my little bit of chicken in the kitchen.

'What are you going on about?' I asked, baffled.

'Don't act stupid, lad. You know what you're doing . . . muscling in on the chicken graft,' he said, waving his finger at me.

I didn't know what to say as I watched him walk away. I was at first stunned, then I became angry. I decided enough was enough. *What the fuck was he talking about? The fuckin' chicken graft? This sort of petty argument could result in someone losing a life*, I thought.

'Hey Bob, I'm fucking sick and tired of the way you talk to me.' I was well past the fight-or-flight stage; fear had long flown out of the door. I could feel my muscles tense and my shoulders hunch into a classic boxer's stance. With fists clenched, I was readying myself for conflict. I read the shock in Bob's face; he wasn't ready to lock horns. All mouth. Up came the 'front'.

'I'm just telling you, OK? End of . . . ' he said as he bounced down the stairs.

'Yeah, end of,' I shouted at his retreating back. I was still fuming but I also felt relieved. It had been coming for a while – standing up to Big Bob had lanced a pernicious boil. The muscle head bounced around dishing out orders like he was some hardcase from the Bronx. I couldn't care less who you thought you were on the outside, I wasn't afraid of anyone. What I was afraid of was who *I* was and what I could do to myself and others. I felt I was being tested by everyone at every opportunity because I was being so passive. I just wanted to change and move forward, but I was also going to let you know I wasn't changing into a bellend, letting bullies and wannabe gangsters walk all over me. Big Bob's attitude changed towards me from then on. I'll say it how it is: don't become someone's victim. No one respects a coward.

There was always somebody complaining about something. I had a pair of grey Nike flip-flops that squeaked every time I walked along the corridors every morning while I got myself ready for the gym. I was always up early and so were the noisy flip-flops.

It was 6.30 a.m. and Gandy popped his head out of the door. His room was a few doors down the corridor from mine and I had to pass his door on my way to the loo.

'Morning, Bill,' he whispered. 'Bob and the lads don't take kindly to the noise you're making with those flippers, lad,' he said, still half asleep.

'I couldn't give a fuck about them. I'm not David Blaine and I can't walk on air,' I said as I walked by with my flip-flops squeaking and squelching. Gandy withdrew, muttering something about not being arsed because he was up early anyway. I liked Gandy and knew he was only giving me a heads up.

The first person to moan about it was Ray. He was probably the most sensitive sleeper on the landing. 'Bill, can I have a quiet word?' he said, ushering me into his pad.

'Yeah. What's up, Ray?' I asked, knowing quite well what was up.

'How are you feeling out of ten? Are you happy?'

'I'm living the dream, full blown ten across the scale,' I said, doing my best to humour him.

'That's good, no that's beautiful, but we need to talk about your flip-flops. Bob, myself and a few others aren't happy. It's waking us up,' Ray said, his arms folded across his skinny chest, nodding as he spoke.

'Oh yeah? What would you suggest, mate?' I asked out of curiosity and with a hint of a smile. I'd had enough of all their bullshit and petty rules. What kind of prison was this? When you can't even go for a piss without waking someone up? Spend a night in a cell with eighty people, sleeping on a floor with one toilet to share and a sea of bodies to climb over every time you needed to relieve yourself, then come back and whine over a pair of flip-flops for fuck's sake!

'Well, we were thinking of a compromise: just a little bit of a curfew on the time you wear them,' he offered, massaging the few black hairs on the end of his chin. He perpetually had the air of a guru contemplating the meaning of life.

I couldn't help it. I burst out laughing but he was deadly serious.

'A curfew? Is this some kind of order handed down by a tribunal?' I could hardly believe the shit I was hearing.

'Yeah, yeah, we were thinking 7 a.m. till 10 a.m. and then 6 p.m. till 8 p.m. That sound good to you?' All said without batting an eyelid. Normal as breathing.

'That sounds absolutely fabulous,' I agreed, stifling my laughter. I walked out of his pad shaking my head in incredulity.

'What's up, Bill?' Gandy asked as I walked past him, still laughing.

'Ask the fucking flip-flop police over there, sending me to court to get a curfew on my flip-flops! It'll be an ASBO next,' I shouted back.

'Yeah, the FBI are about in force tonight, Bill,' he said.

I only had weeks to go before my release, so I started to detach myself from the rest of the inmates, to keep safe. I quickly found myself feeling isolated and not a part of the prison population, which was fine by me. I kept in touch with friends and family regularly by phone and received a visit at least once a week. It was always awkward having visits. There was never much to say and most of the time was just spent staring at everyone else's visitors and checking out if there were any fit birds. I only enjoyed the first thirty minutes because that consisted of me getting a few goodies from the prison canteen. My mates would ask me what it was like being in an open prison, so I told them: 'I am in a jail full of lick-arses, grasses, shitbags and bullies. Some of them would love to see you get shipped out and robbed of your liberty.'

Every night I could hear them on their smuggled prison phones, screaming at girlfriends, making demands and threats. I'd had no contact with a female for over a year and felt better for being single. No Facebook or any kind of social media, just plenty of writing and training. I could see the emotional upheaval and even hear it through the breeze blocks between cells each evening. Some men couldn't cope with the ending of a relationship and would make a run for the hills. It was easy to abscond, no locked gates, no bars, and freedom only a few hundred feet away. Absconding would cost you an extra six months added to your sentence and you would lose the chance of ever getting to an open jail. I was just glad it was all coming to an end. I'd had enough of prison and the petty dramas it created. If I was serving any longer, I'd have made a break for it myself before I ended up losing the plot. Only I knew how lucky I was to be here . . . something I constantly reminded myself of. Don't jeopardise a good thing!

We are privileged in the UK to have the opportunity to reach places such as Thorn Cross – a low-level prison where you are called by your first name and treated like a human being.

I am convinced society would benefit if the justice system could find a way to open up more of these types of prisons. It's not about rehabilitation, it's about humanising individuals who have been institutionalised and who have had their social skills reduced to base-level survival mode – prisoners who are about to be ejected back into the outside world, often placed in hostels miles from their families, and expected to cope with very little in the way of support. Even the most egregious, the most hopeless, deserve a chance to rebuild their lives as they head towards release – if only to protect their own communities. We tend to lock people up and throw away the key until it's their time for release, meaning an individual, full of bitter resentment for any kind of authority owing to the treatment they have received, is back on the streets desperate for money and usually drugs.

I know from years of experience that being treated like an animal will mean you behave as such – but having been given the chance to come here had given me hope. It taught me that the prison service does have the ability to genuinely reform inmates. It is just a shame there are so few Cat D establishments available and that those who are placed in Cat D are handpicked with a bias for those already exhibiting good behaviour. The addicted who really need to be treated with love and professional care are constantly locked up in the harshest conditions, perpetuating their addictions and behavioural problems.

Time seemed to slow down the closer it got to my release. The weeks, the days, even the hours seemed to go on forever but here it was – Christmas Eve and I was going home. The sheer relief as I stepped through those gates for the last time and headed into freedom. I couldn't wait to see my mum, my family and especially my brother Joseph. It was over. I had managed to make it without having to use drugs as a way of escaping. Anything was possible now. When we surrender from the heart we never have to fight again.

Hereafter

If you can look into the seeds of time,
And say which grain will grow and which will not;
Speak then to me.

> *Macbeth* Act 1, Scene 3,
> William Shakespeare

YOUTH means rarely having to face our own mortality. Add physical strength, a keen mind, a sense of adventure and powerful experiences of trauma, and the unfolding story of my life was perhaps always going to be unpredictable, and often extreme. There is always a sense of there being more time, no matter how bad the situation is, and time offers a sense of hope. Once you pass forty, and head towards a half century in this world, your own mortality is staring you in the face. With my own particular health problems, it has never looked away. Death keeps me firmly in its gaze, but that has helped me come to terms with the past and look forward to the future.

So far, I have had a disordered existence. Trust me when I say that being in prison and missing my own film premieres will never leave me. But whether behind bars or walking the streets as a free man, you are always imprisoned if you live in fear, at odds with others, and being controlled by an addiction that will bring the strongest man to his knees.

I would like to say I am in a place where I am grateful for all of my experiences in life so far but, at this stage of my journey, I am still at the beginning of a work-in-progress where the simple joys of what I would have once considered an everyday existence are now a source of contentment and growth, whether it be a session at the gym or a coffee with a mate. Along the way, I am lucky to have met some inspirational people whose instincts were to believe in me. They have stuck around long enough to provide me with invaluable, ongoing support and encouragement: I would like to prove their instincts about me were correct.

It is impossible to live without hurting others, and I cannot guarantee I never will again, but I know the sense of strength and hope that comes from simply helping another human being in the most basic ways. Such acts are now my building blocks for the future, while I work out what to do next with my life.

So, what would I like to do next? Do any of us really know the answer to that question? I know that my personality might crave excitement and adventure, but there are other ways of quenching that thirst without ending up in the depths of despair. As for being happy, at the moment I would settle for peace, contentment and a chance to repair fractured relationships as well the opportunity to build further meaningful ones.

I never thought in my lowest moments that there was a future for me, but the fact that I am still here means that someone, somewhere, has bigger plans for me and I am happy to make my way in life through quiet improvements rather than giant leaps.

I have moved right out of the gutter and I am standing on the pavement now, back in the real world, passing others as I go, my back straight and my mind focused.

But my head isn't set forwards, I am keeping it firmly up; in that way I am always looking at the stars.

Acknowledgements

I would like to thank everyone who was involved in the writing of this book. Your words of encouragement and guidance made all the difference. And I'd especially like to thank my publisher, Duncan Proudfoot, for taking the chance and Amanda Keats for pulling it all together.

Index

Air (Chiang Mai Central Prison inmate) 159–61
alcohol addiction 130, 131
Alcoholics Anonymous (AA) 51, 133
Alf (drugs unit manager) 40, 41
Ali the Iranian (Chiang Mai Central Prison inmate) 161
Ali, Muhammad 22, 91
Altitude Films 188–9
Anderson, Paul 'Boycey' 104
Anne (drugs worker) 34
arsonists 167
Ash (mentor) 48–9
Austie (cat burglar) 147

Barrett, Syd 46
Barry-the-handbag 13–14
Benn, Nigel 23
Bernie (Billy's lodger) 125
Big Bob (Thorn Cross prison cleaner) 244–6
Big George (Billy's friend) 113–15
Boulter, Roy (Hurricane Films manager) 59–63, 65, 73–4, 104
Bournemouth 7–11, 13, 27
Brandon (drug user) 38, 45
Bristol 31

Broadgreen Hospital 82
Bruno, Frank 23

cannabis 34, 103–5, 119–20, 131, 137, 171, 190, 198, 207
Cannes Film Festival 1–2, 97, 110–11, 115, 123
Caroline (rehab client) 131–2
Catherine (Parisienne guide) 72
Cebu prison, Philippines 92, 96–7
  dancing inmates 89, 96
Channel 4 News 188, 189–90, 216, 236
Chiang Mai Central Prison, Thailand 6–8, 11–12, 63, 65, 83, 89–96, 149, 156–61, 168–9, 182, 191–3, 202–4, 216–18, 227–8
Claire (ex-user) 142–3
cocaine 130, 142–3, 171, 175
  see also crack cocaine
Cocks, Mr 208
Cole, Finn 104
Cole, Joe 73–4, 92, 93, 104
Colin (Billy's friend) 173–4
Connor, Mr (teacher) 19
crack cocaine 2, 33, 101–2, 110, 118–21, 221

Crown Court 142, 143

Dagher, Rita 71–2, 96, 97, 125
dark web 105
David (doctor) 82–3
Davis, Mr 5, 6, 7
Dean (drug user) 42
Depp, Johnny 37
Derek (publisher) 58, 61
dialectical behavioural therapy (DBT) 131, 133
diazepam 94, 100
Diesel, Vin 93
Donaldson, Paul 195–8
Driscoll (doorman) 179
Dublin Film Festival 140, 142
Duran, Robert 'Hands of Stone' 23

Ebby (Billy's friend) 101–2
Ecstasy 174, 175
Eddie (volunteer) 46
Egypt 67
Elizabeth (rehab client) 137
Essex 127
Eubank, Chris 23

Farm, The 61
Fast and Furious, The movies 93
Fat Controller (Sam's son) 67
Foster, Judge 150–1
Francesca (Billy's girlfriend) 81–2
Frank (Billy's Grandfather) 20
Freddie, Uncle 18–19

Gandy (Thorn Cross inmate) 245–7
Gary (Billy's cousin) 103, 104, 105, 120
Gateway Recovery Centre, The 125–6, 127–35, 137–8, 139
'Genie in the Gutter' (charity) 62
Geordie (HMP Hindley inmate) 210, 222–5, 227

George (rehab client) 130, 137
Gogg (Chiang Mai Central Prison inmate) 192–3
Goulding, Officer 8
Graham, Stephen 104
Green, Professor 188, 189, 208

Hamish (Altitude Films worker) 188
Hannah (Thorn Cross guard) 241–2
Helen (area manager) 64–5
heroin 13, 27, 33, 40, 47–9, 100–2, 110, 121, 126, 128–30, 171, 190, 209, 221
HMP Hindley 204–5, 207–11, 213–19, 221–7, 229, 232–8, 240–1
HMP Liverpool 145–8, 151–9, 162–3, 165–72, 173–84, 185–99, 201–2, 204–7, 244
  as dispersal prison 205–6
  drugs problem 156, 158–9, 165–6, 171–2, 185–6, 190–1, 193, 195–6
HMP Manchester (Strangeways) 56
HMP Risley 204
HMP Stafford 12–13, 168, 195
HMP Wandsworth 5–9, 11–12, 13
Hunnam, Charlie 71, 73
Hurricane Films 57–8, 59–61, 125, 127, 139

Imelda (drug user) 42
Independent (newspaper) 188, 190
Inside Time (prison newspaper) 236
Irish Republican Army (IRA) 56
Ismalone, David 93

Jack (HMP Liverpool inmate) 191, 192
Jackson, Michael 89, 96
Jason (HMP Liverpool inmate) 187
Jay (Billy's friend) 8–11, 104
Jenkins, Terry 12–13
John (Billy's friend) 66

John (Billy's friend's father) 85
John (boxing coach) 22
John (Thorn Cross inmate) 240
Johnny Mad Dog (film, 2008) 62–3
Jom (Chiang Mai Central Prison inmate) 159–61
Joyce, Tommy 183–4

Kamsing, Sonrak 93
'kangaroo courts' 141
Karen (drug dealer/user) 121–2
Kathleen (missionary) 159
Kenny (Billy's neighbour) 136
Kevin White Unit, Liverpool 34–46
Klong Prem prison, Bangkok 157–8, 193, 202–4, 216
knife crime 231

LaBeouf, Shia 73
Laura (therapist) 37–8, 40, 43–4
Lawrence (lifer) 244
Lawrence (rehab client) 135
Leanne (drug worker) 33
Lee (Billy's friend) 114
Leon (HMP Hindley inmate) 229–31
Leonard, Sugar Ray 23
Linda McCartney Centre 241–2
Lisa (HMP Liverpool offender manager) 189
Liverpool 2, 12, 25, 27, 30, 34, 57, 60–1, 64, 74, 115, 127, 134, 204, 231, 243–4
Liverpool Crown Court 148
Liverpool Echo (newspaper) 188, 190, 236
lofexidine 36
LSD (lysergic acid diethylamide) 26

Mac (HMP Liverpool biohazard cleaner) 166, 168, 206
magistrates 141

Marco (Cebu prison governor) 92, 96
Mark (Billy's housemate) 68
Mark (HMP Liverpool recovery mentor) 187
Martin, Colin 104
Mason, Mr ('Pit Bull') 197–8
Matt D (HMP Liverpool inmate) 162
Maverick House, Dublin 61, 64
Max (HMP Hindley inmate) 222–3, 224, 227
McGarrick, Mrs 24–5
Megan (Billy's niece) 52–3
Merseyside 63, 149
methadone 29, 30, 34, 41–2, 94, 207–8
Mike (addiction worker) 63–4, 65
Mishka (drug user) 44–5
Miss D (HMP Liverpool head cleaner) 162–3, 169–70, 183, 184
Molly (drug user) 38–9
Moon, Mr (prison officer) 157, 158
Moore, Anthony (Billy's younger brother) 15, 18, 20
Moore, Billy
  and addiction 11–13, 27, 29–32, 47–9, 62–3, 75, 87, 93–6, 148–50
    attempts at detox following relapse 109–11, 115
    cannabis oil use 103–5
    clean but tempted in HMP Liverpool 171–2
    clean in HMP Hindley 208
    cold turkey in HMP Hindley 205
    in coma after taking pills 154
    drug driving charge 140–1
    grows cannabis farm 105, 119–20
    guilt and shame of 137
    on hurting the ones you love 233–4

leaves The Gateway Recovery Centre 137–8, 139–40

rehabilitation at The Gateway Recovery Centre 125–6, 127–35, 137–8

relapse after fifty-six days clean 115, 117–25

relapse due to prescription drug use after five years clean 99–105, 107–9

resorts to burglary to fund habit 124, 135–6, 140, 142–4, 148–51, 170, 189–90

spiritual relapse 78

on taking the decision to get clean 30–2, 33–46

atheism 49

books, *A Prayer Before Dawn* (2011) 58–60, 64–5, 93, 149

boxing 20, 21–4, 89–92

cancer diagnosis, non-Hodgkin's lymphoma 81–7, 93, 97, 99, 102–5, 107–11, 149

  chemotherapy 102–3, 108, 141

  effect on his loved ones 102

  remission 111, 150, 241–2

  Sol and Roy organise benefit night in aid of 104–5

character

  angry 28

  ego 60, 74, 77–9

  emotionally damaged 48–9

  fear of loneliness 49–50, 62, 101, 120, 123, 232

  inner emptiness 68–9, 78

  karma 80

  low self-esteem 49, 60

  need for more 69

  need to feel superior 120

  never given the psychological space to mature 145

  obsessive 34

  self-destructive 12, 125

  self-hatred 28

  see also Moore, Billy, mental health

charity work 62, 63

childhood 14–15, 17–26

  boxing 20, 21–4

  crime 21, 25–6, 27

  drink 24

  drugs 21, 24, 26, 27

  ear injury 26

  in the Royal Artillery cadets 23

  suffers physical abuse 20–1, 22, 24–6, 39, 43–4

on fame 77–8

film of his life made, *A Prayer Before Dawn* (2017) 60–4, 71–4, 77–8, 82–3, 89, 92–3, 96–7, 104, 110–11, 115, 123, 140, 149

  Billy's cameo role as his father in 92, 97

  money matters 241

  release 216, 251–2

  run up to release 188–90, 205, 208

on the future 251–3

gets paid job working with addiction 63–5, 149

  nominated for recovery worker of the year 68

and his father's death 26, 66, 71, 97

and his father's diagnosis of cancer 65–6

and Hurricane Films 57–8, 59–63

knife possession charge 140–2

meets up with his mum after HMP Wandsworth stay 17, 27–8

mental health 149

  depression 103, 149

  Post-Traumatic Stress Disorder 149, 150

sectioned under the Mental
Health Act 149–50
suicide attempts 149
and money matters 75, 102, 123–4,
241
on mortality 251
moves in with mum following
HMP Wandsworth stay 28
prison career
and addiction 48
and boxing 89–92
in Chiang Mai Central Prison
6–8, 11–12, 63, 65, 83, 89–96,
149, 156–61, 182, 191–3, 202–
4, 216–18, 227–8
isolation 168–9
in HMP Hindley 204–5, 207–
11, 213–19, 221–7, 229, 232–8,
240–1
in HMP Liverpool 145–8,
151–4, 155–9, 162–3, 165–72,
173–84, 185–99, 205–7, 244
drugs problem 156, 158–9,
165–6, 171–2, 185–6,
190–1, 193, 195–6
leads roof riot 145–8
Northwest Tornado Team
visits 194–5, 198–9
prison transfer 201–2, 204
in HMP Stafford 12–13, 168,
195
in HMP Wandsworth
encouraged to write a book
13
job as gym orderly 5
receives counselling 11–12
release 5–9
in Klong Prem prison 157–8,
193, 202–4, 216
in Thorn Cross Category D
prison 236–8, 239–49
release 249

rock bottom 123–5
romantic relationships 12, 46–8,
74–5, 77–9, 99
Francesca 81–2
Olivia 108–11, 117–20, 125, 127,
137, 139, 142–3, 186–7, 208,
215–16, 232–3, 236
Samantha 48–52, 53–6, 58–9,
61, 66–8, 71, 77
social media followers 60, 74
Toxteth knife attack on 231–2
Moore, Joe (Billy's younger brother)
15, 28, 243, 249
Moore, Kelly (Billy's sister) 15, 20,
241, 242
Moore, Kevin (Billy's brother) 15, 65
Moore, Lisa (Billy's sister) 15, 26,
51–2, 65, 66
Moore, Pat (Billy's mum) 14, 17–19,
23, 135, 241, 243
and A Prayer Before Dawn (film) 59,
60
and Billy's addiction 31, 126
and Billy's cancer diagnosis 85–7
and Billy's father's cancer 65
and Billy's girlfriend Samantha 50,
66, 68
and Billy's incarceration in HMP
Liverpool 152–4
as Billy's number one fan 60
and Billy's release from Thorn
Cross 249
and her mother's death 8
leaves Billy's father Tony 52
and Purple Aki 55–6
suffers domestic violence at the
hands of Billy's father 14–15,
17–18, 20, 26
Moore, Tony (Billy's father) 19–21,
23–7
cancer 65–6
death 26, 66, 71, 97

drinking 14, 20, 26, 52, 66
gambling 14
life in a hostel 52–3
street drinker 52
tries to make amends for his ways
   in later years 51–2
violent nature 14–15, 19–22, 24–6,
   39, 43–4
Morgan, Piers 206
morphine sulphate 129

Nan (prison boxing trainer) 90–2, 93
Narcotics Anonymous 30–1, 51, 149,
   205, 225
National Offender Management
   System (NOMS) 157
Neil (therapist) 130, 132, 137
Nicole (Hurricane Films worker)
   57–8, 59
Nigel (HMP Hindley inmate) 222–3

Olivia (Billy's girlfriend) 108–11,
   117–20, 125, 127, 137, 139, 142–3,
   186–7, 208, 215–16, 232–3, 236
opiates 93, 99–100, 101, 109, 114,
   149, 233

Papadopoulos, Sol (Hurricane Films
   manager) 59–60, 62–3, 65, 73–4,
   104
Paris 71–3
Passenger 233
Pauline (therapist) 134
Peaky Blinders (TV series) 73, 74, 104
Philippines 89, 92, 92–3, 96, 96–7
Pink Floyd 46
Podge (Billy's friend) 29–32, 68
Pon (Thai prison inmate) 90–2
Prayer Before Dawn, A (film, 2017)
   60–4, 71–4, 77–8, 82–3, 89, 92–3,
   96–7, 104, 110–11, 115, 123, 140,
   149, 241

Billy's cameo role as his father in
   92, 97
release 216, 251–2
run up to the release of 188–90,
   205, 208
Prayer Before Dawn, A (Moore, 2011)
   58–60, 64–5, 93, 149
pregabalin 122
Prisit (Chiang Mai Central Prison
   guard) 169, 218
Purple Aki 55–6

Rambo IV (film, 2008) 23
Ray (Thorn Cross prison mentor)
   239–40, 242–3, 246
Red (HMP Liverpool orderly) 166,
   168
Richardson, Miss 5–7
Ritchie (drug user) 44–5
Rob (friend of Big George) 113–15
Robbo (HMP Liverpool inmate) 175,
   178–9, 195
Rocky movies 23
Rodgers, Mr 237
Ronnie (drug dealer/user) 121–2
Rosie (tomcat) 67–8
Royal University Hospital, Liverpool
   154
Ryan (HMP Hindley inmate) 234

St Ambrose ABC boxing club
   21–2
Saltrese, Nick 61–2
Samantha (Billy's girlfriend) 48–56,
   58–9, 61, 66–8, 71, 77
   aborts their child 50, 51, 53, 58
Sandy (therapist) 128, 131, 133–4,
   141
Sauvaire, Jean-Stéphane 62–3, 71,
   73–4, 92, 93, 97
Scott (Chiang Mai Central Prison
   inmate) 168–9

Shakespeare, William 5, 17, 29, 33, 47, 57, 71, 77, 81, 89, 99, 107, 113, 117, 127, 139, 145, 155, 165, 173, 185, 201, 213, 221, 229, 239, 251
Shannon (ex-user) 142–3
Sharm el-Sheikh 67
Smith, 'Bonecrusher' 22
Smith, Doctor 85
Smooth, Mr 208
Snowy (club worker) 10
spice 156, 159, 165, 171, 185–6, 198, 213–14, 216
Spinks, Leon 22
Stallone, Sylvester 23
Ste the E (HMP Liverpool inmate) 174–9, 183–4, 188, 194, 198
Subutex 109, 128
Sue (doctor) 82

Thailand 6–8, 11–12, 59, 63, 65, 82–3, 86, 89–93, 149, 156–9, 180, 182, 188, 191–3, 207, 216–18, 227–8
Thatcher, Margaret 23
Thorn Cross Category D prison 236–8, 239–49
Thoroughgoode, Mr 11–12
Tom (rehab client) 129, 137

Tomaz 'Seb the Lithuanian machine' (HMP Liverpool inmate) 206–7
Tommy (Billy's friend) 241
Tony (HMP Liverpool inmate) 177–8
Toxteth, Liverpool 231
tramadol 126, 159, 168
Tyson, Mike 22–3

Vidal, Gore 225
Vito the Frog 9–10

Walla (Pat's husband/Billy's step-father) 65–6, 135
Waterstones 64–5
Watson, Michael 23
Whiston Hospital 65
Wilde, Oscar 2
Will (Billy's friend) 139
Willo (Thorn Cross prison mentor) 239, 240

Xanax 94

ya ba (drug) 94
Offender (film, 2012) 73
Yozza (rehab client) 35–41, 44–5